A
Verse
a Day
for the
Anxious
Soul

A
Verse
a Day
for the
Anxious
Soul

---

100 Days of Peace for the Calm You Crave

Becky Keife

FOREWORD BY JENNIFER TUCKER

WaterBrook

WaterBrook

An imprint of the Penguin Random House Christian Publishing Group,
a division of Penguin Random House LLC

1745 Broadway, New York, NY 10019

waterbrookmultnomah.com
penguinrandomhouse.com

Library of Congress Cataloging-in-Publication Data

Names: Keife, Becky author
Title: A verse a day for the anxious soul : 100 days of peace for the calm you crave / Becky Keife.
Description: First edition. | New York, NY : WaterBrook, an imprint of the Penguin Random House Christian Publishing Group, a division of Penguin Random House LLC, [2025] | Includes bibliographical references.
Identifiers: LCCN 2025009574 | ISBN 9780593602713 hardcover | ISBN 9780593602720 ebook
Subjects: LCSH: Peace of mind—Religious aspects—Christianity—Prayers and devotions | Anxiety—Religious aspects—Christianity—Prayers and devotions | LCGFT: Devotional literature | Prayers
Classification: LCC BV4908.5 .K447 2025 | DDC 242/.2—dc23/eng/20250716
LC record available at https://lccn.loc.gov/2025009574

Printed in the United States of America on acid-free paper

2nd Printing

First Edition

The authorized representative in the EU for product safety and compliance is Penguin Random House Ireland, Morrison Chambers, 32 Nassau Street, Dublin D02 YH68, Ireland. https://eu-contact.penguin.ie

BOOK TEAM: Editor: Jamie Lapeyrolerie • Production editor: Jessica Choi • Managing editor: Julia Wallace • Production manager: Jane Sankner • Copy editor: Bailey Utecht • Proofreaders: Tracey Moore, Karissa Silvers

Book design by Jo Anne Metsch

For details on special quantity discounts for bulk purchases, contact
specialmarketscms@penguinrandomhouse.com.

To Elise Marie,
thank you for always pointing me to the goodness of God.
Of all the people on the planet . . .

To the ones who have suffered in silence,
you are not alone.
Hope is here.

Foreword

For a long time, I saw anxiety as an enemy I had to overcome and a frustrating roadblock to my faith. I masked it beneath layers of perfectionism, overworking, and people-pleasing. I would read verses about it and feel judgment and shame. Passages like "Be anxious for nothing" (Philippians 4:6), "Do not worry about your life" (Matthew 6:25), and the hundreds of times we're reminded, "Don't be afraid" (Deuteronomy 31:6), "Don't be afraid" (John 14:27), "Don't be afraid" (Isaiah 41:10) all felt like words of condemnation to my struggling soul.

I couldn't reconcile what God said about anxiety in Scripture with the very real and persistent symptoms of anxiety that continued to plague my days, no matter how hard I tried or how much I prayed. I just wanted anxiety to go away so that I could experience the joy and peace I so longed for.

But sometimes, the hard thing we don't want is the very thing God can use to turn our hearts toward him. Sometimes, the things we think are keeping us from experiencing peace and rest are the very things God can use to draw us closer to the source of peace himself.

It turns out, anxiety isn't our enemy. And those verses that once felt like condemnation from a harsh judge are actually words of comfort from a loving Father.

God is not mad at us for being anxious, and he isn't waiting to strike us down because we're afraid. He knows we will experience anxiety and worry and fear—these are common human emotions. He simply comes to us with unwavering compassion and lovingly reminds us, "You don't *have* to be afraid. Just come to me. I'm with you, and I'll take care of you. You are safe and held and loved."

It turns out, the limitations we feel are holding us back are actually invitations to draw closer to Christ.

The anxiety we think is an obstacle to our faith is actually an opportunity to experience even deeper peace than we ever imagined possible.

Becky knows this in a profoundly personal way. She has walked this journey. She knows the struggle. And she is a kind and trusted guide helping our anxious souls experience the peace and calm that we so desperately crave.

Whatever your story, however great your anxiety or deep your pain, the truth is:

There are arms that can hold your heart when everything is falling apart.

There is a voice that can calm your fears when anxiety is pressing in.

There are wings that can shelter your soul when the storms of suffering rain down.

And there is a place where shame fades away and hope holds fast, where peace covers the darkness, where calm can fill your soul, and where you can find real rest.

Through the pages of this book, Becky will guide you to that place. She will gently lead you into the open arms of Jesus—right into the center of his presence where there is safety and refuge and help in times of anxiety, worry, and despair.

You don't *have* to be afraid. You don't *have* to worry.

Jesus is here.

You are safe and held and loved.

—JENNIFER TUCKER
Author of *Breath as Prayer* and *Present in Prayer*

Contents

Foreword by Jennifer Tucker vii
Introduction: Hope for Your Anxious Soul xv

 1 Stop Carrying It All Alone 2
 2 God's Help for the Engine in My Chest 4
 3 Go to Bed and Take the B 6
 4 The Beauty of "And" 8
 5 Longing for Home 10
 6 Keep Crying Out for Mercy 12
 7 Don't Wait to Deserve It 14

PEACE PRACTICE #1: MOVE 16

 8 Empathy Overload 18
 9 You Belong to God, Not Fear 20
10 Stop Stuffing Grief in the Closet 22
11 Jesus Will Come for You 24
12 A New Way of Thinking 26
13 The Badge of Weariness 28
14 The Bigger Picture of Anxiety 30

PEACE PRACTICE #2: CONNECT 32

15 Stupid Mistakes and God's Perfect Love 34
16 The First Step Toward Freedom 36
17 Expectations vs. Expectancy 38

18 Rethinking Our Thorns 40
19 Desperate to Understand 42
20 When You're at the End of Your Rope 44
21 The Real Purpose of Fear 46

PEACE PRACTICE #3: JOURNAL 48

22 The Ultimate Invitation 50
23 Could Your Anxiety Be a Gift? 52
24 Wisdom for Every Need 54
25 Jesus Comes Near 56
26 Worth the Wait 58
27 Receive the Rest You Need 60
28 Tangled and Ready for Rescue 62

PEACE PRACTICE #4: CRY 64

29 The Master Upcycler 66
30 Soul Refreshment 68
31 The Answer You Can Count On 70
32 When You Don't Want to Miss His Voice 72
33 Let Them See You Cry 74
34 Don't Get Drunk on Worry 76
35 When All You Feel Is Pain and Fear 78

PEACE PRACTICE #5: GET OUTSIDE 80

36 Tell God the Truth 82
37 New Life for Dry Bones 84
38 The Continual Makeover 86
39 Put Jesus in the Picture 88
40 You're Never Really Alone 90
41 The Unwanted Cup 92
42 Beauty from Prickly Places 94

PEACE PRACTICE #6: HUG 96

43 Anxiety Pinball 98
44 Better Than Caffeine 100
45 Good News When Plans Fail 102
46 Untangling Anxiety Through Pen and Prayer 104
47 The Teeter-Totter of Fine and Unfine 106
48 Decision Paralysis 108
49 When You Keep Spraining That Ankle 110

PEACE PRACTICE #7: REST 112

50 Unseen Spiderwebs 114
51 Let Peace Be Your Teacher 116
52 God Loves What He Made 118
53 Crave This 120
54 It's Time to Share Your Struggles 122
55 What Only God Can Do 124
56 Hope for Sorrow and Failure 126

PEACE PRACTICE #8: LAUGH 128

57 The Best Way to Start Your Day 130
58 Combatting Spiritual Cynicism 132
59 Helicopter Brain 134
60 No Caveats or Conditions 136
61 Lemon Orzo Soup and Asking for Help 138
62 The Gift of Repentance 140
63 The Battle for Your Heart 142

PEACE PRACTICE #9: ENGAGE 144

64 When You Are Afraid 146
65 Before You Hide or Push Through 148
66 Grace for Every Accusation 150

67 You Don't Have to Explain It to God 152
68 The World Would Never Tell You to Do This 154
69 What Worry Adds Up To 156
70 When You're Barely Hanging On 158

PEACE PRACTICE #10: UNPLUG 160

71 You Are Cared For and Carried 162
72 On Earth as It Is in Heaven 164
73 Honesty, Overwhelm, and Hearing God's Voice 166
74 One Thing to Do Today (and Every Day) 168
75 Stop Drinking Soul Poison 170
76 The Gap We Try to Fill 172
77 Jesus Isn't Afraid of Your Dirt 174

PEACE PRACTICE #11: SERVE 176

78 When the Day Already Feels Like Too Much 178
79 Flip the Script 180
80 You Don't Have to Save Yourself 182
81 Asking *What* Instead of *Why* 184
82 Pulled Apart 186
83 From Wallowing to Receiving 188
84 Do You See Jesus? 190

PEACE PRACTICE #12: GIVE THANKS 192

85 Tap, Tap, Tap 194
86 Moved with Compassion 196
87 True Life After Dashed Dreams 198
88 Don't Write Off Rest 200
89 King Jesus and Toilet Conversions 202
90 Trusting God with Soup 204
91 Hope in the Wilderness 206

PEACE PRACTICE #13: REFUEL 208

92 Gratitude in the Grind 210
93 Keep Confessing Your Fears 212
94 Margot Makes Me Smile 214
95 Faith That Sings in the Dark 216
96 Don't Skip the Banana 218
97 For the Forgotten and Overlooked 220
98 Heart Surgery 222

PEACE PRACTICE #14: PRAY 224

 99 Who Do You Want to Be? 226
100 The Way Forward 228

   With Gratitude 231
   Notes 233

Introduction

Hope for Your Anxious Soul

For years I didn't know what was happening to me. I didn't understand why I would go to bed with a racing mind or wake up feeling like there was a brick on my chest. I didn't know why I often carried a deep sadness that didn't match my circumstances. Why was my body tense and my thoughts scattered and my heart so knotted up with grief and worry? And why did those knots seem to stack together in a wall of pain and irritation that kept me feeling distant from God and the people I love?

For years I didn't know that I struggled with anxiety.

I thought that if I just prayed more, tried harder, or managed my time better, then *I* would be better. I believed my anxiety was my own scarlet A, the mark of a weak or faithless Christian. Surely if I just trusted God more, then I wouldn't feel this way. Struggling with anxiety felt like an indictment on my character and something that I needed to fix—*stat*!

Eventually I discovered that not only was my anxiety a legitimate diagnosis—worthy of intervention and support just like any physical malady—but in many ways it was also a gift.

How could I possibly consider anxiety a *gift*? Because it was what led me to experience more of God's powerful presence, tangible grace, and practical strength.

I've spent years finding a trustworthy path toward healthy coping, peace, and healing. This path has looked like getting radically honest about my struggles, going to therapy, and taking medication when needed. I thank God for tools and resources to address the physical and psychological aspects of anxiety.

But anxiety is something that not only impacts the body and mind—it also affects the soul. Whether you relate to the ways anxiety manifests for me or not, you probably deal with anxious feelings on some level. From everyday stress and worry to a clinical diagnosis, the continuum of anxiety impacts everyone.

When your soul is anxious, it's hard to trust God and remember his promises. When your soul is anxious, it's easy to feel discouraged, defeated, and utterly alone. An anxious soul is like a tornado of worry and what-ifs swirling at breakneck speed on a highway of destruction—able to shatter your confidence, splinter your relationships, and flatten your faith. But what if an anxious soul wasn't a terror to hide from but an opportunity to draw closer to God?

That angsty, knotted-up, restless feeling is there not to shame you but to usher you toward the One you really need. In my most anxious moments, the only place I've found true rest, relief, and restoration for my soul is in the presence of Jesus.

Jesus says, "Come to me, all of you who are weary and carry heavy burdens, and I will give you rest. Take my yoke upon you. Let me teach you, because I am humble and gentle at heart, and you will find rest for your souls. For my yoke is easy to bear, and the burden I give you is light" (Matthew 11:28–30).

Come. That's the invitation. And whom does Jesus invite to come? *All who are weary and burdened.* That's me. And that's you. Do you see the freedom here? Jesus *expects* us to be weary and burdened! He knows that as imperfect people living in a broken world, we are going to be weighed down by worry and anxiety. He doesn't condemn us for it; he offers to carry the burden with us.

As we accept Jesus's invitation to come to him, we also get to *learn* from him. We can learn how to stop relying on our own faltering strength and start depending on his steadfast care. We can stop trying to control our lives and master our anxiety and instead surrender it all to God and *find rest* for our anxious souls.

Yes, this gift is real, and you can start experiencing it one day at a time.

WHAT YOU'LL FIND IN THIS BOOK

A Verse a Day for the Anxious Soul is a gentle guide that will help you encounter the life-changing presence of Jesus. Like the title promises, every day you'll discover a **verse** to soothe and encourage your anxious soul. Don't just glance at these verses—linger on them. Try reading the daily verse aloud, write it in your journal, underline it in your physical Bible, or look it up in a different translation. The point is to *engage* with God's Word! (It's okay if you're not accustomed to reading the Bible. I'll be walking with you, and God's got something for you!) Scripture is our soul's oxygen—essential, life-giving, and sustaining.

Each verse is followed by a short **devotion.** This is where I get to come alongside you as a fellow anxiety wrestler and share soul-steadying truth that always leads back to Jesus. We'll dig into a scripture together, and I'll share what it means in a way that's clear, relatable, and exactly what I needed when my anxiety was spiraling out of control.

Next, you'll find a simple exercise to **inhale truth** and **exhale trust.** This practice combines the physiological benefits of breath regulation with the spiritual benefits of Scripture meditation. When you inhale truth and exhale trust, God's Word will sink deeper into your mind and soul, providing long-lasting peace and strength. I recommend inhaling slowly for four counts, holding for four counts, exhaling for four counts, and pausing for four counts. (This is often referred to as box breathing or square breathing.) Do this three times. Or follow the inhale-exhale prompts in whatever way feels best to you.

Lastly, you'll reflect and talk to God through a written **prayer.** Sometimes when we're knotted up with anxiety or overwhelmed by difficult circumstances, it can be hard to know what to pray. I've been there. So borrow these words and make them your own. Each prayer will set you on a path of peace and growth as you come to Jesus, trust him to help carry your load, and receive his gift of rest for your soul.

Throughout the book, you'll also find fourteen **Peace Practices**— simple, down-to-earth ways to shift from stress and anxiety to peace and calm. Since anxiety affects our bodies, minds, and souls, these practical tools will help you create new habits and healthy rhythms to ease anxiety and bring balance to every part of your life.

The devotions are numbered for your convenience, but there's no pressure to rush through one hundred days in a row. These pages are here to help you trust in Jesus, to rest and connect with him. So move at the pace that feels right for you.

We can let anxiety make us feel disqualified from closeness with God, or we can let it be the catalyst for greater intimacy with him. In taking just a few intentional minutes a day, your soul can transform from a storm of fear, worry, and overwhelm into a sanctuary of God's powerful peace.

You don't have to stay knotted up in anxiety. There is hope, and it's available to you right now.

I've reached the point in my life where I refuse to face life in my own strength. In fact, I can't. I need Jesus—desperately. Let's seek him together, with open hearts and a renewed sense of purpose. The peace we're longing for is within reach.

Before You Begin

Friend, I am not a doctor, therapist, or psychologist. This book is not intended to diagnose or treat clinical anxiety. As we'll explore in the pages ahead, some kinds of anxiety are common to all people—situational anxiety, daily overwhelm, occasional worry. But anxiety can also persist outside the threshold of typical stress.

If your anxiety is severe, please seek professional help. I've logged many hours talking to a physician and a counselor about my anxiety disorder. There is no shame in needing immediate intervention or ongoing support.

If you are in intense emotional distress, feel mentally unsafe, or are considering harming yourself, please call or text 988. The Suicide & Crisis Lifeline is available 24-7. Conversations are free and confidential.

Please don't suffer alone. Help is available.

You are worthy of support and healing.

Your life matters. You are so loved.

A
Verse
a Day
for the
Anxious
Soul

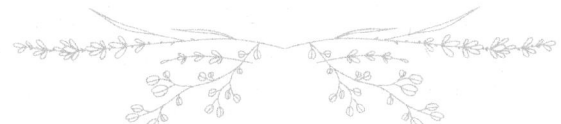

1

Stop Carrying It All Alone

Praise the Lord; praise God our savior!
For each day he carries us in his arms.
—PSALM 68:19

God gave me a mental picture that I never want to forget. In it I was carrying a heavy, heavy load. It was piled up so high that I could barely balance it. I struggled to take even a small step forward. I was utterly weighed down and discouraged.

Then I realized that Jesus was standing right next to me. He opened his arms as an invitation to take what I was carrying. One by one, I handed him my burdens. I gave him the heaviness of my anxiety, a difficult relationship, a source of deep pain, an impossible decision.

Somehow, what I struggled to carry with two arms Jesus now held easily with one. Then he put his other arm around my shoulder. In that moment I knew that even if my circumstances never changed, I didn't have to stay crushed by their weight.

With Jesus by my side, I was no longer stuck.

Though I cannot literally see Jesus next to me, this mental picture reminds me that I always have access to his Spirit's very real presence. God dwells in us, which means he's even closer than an arm around our shoulders.

If you're struggling to carry it all—whatever your "all" may be—that's okay. You actually were never meant to do the carrying. Today you can give your heavy load to Jesus. You can accept the indwelling strength of

God's Spirit. He is the only one capable of holding your burdens and helping you take the next step.

Inhale Truth
Jesus comes to my rescue.

Exhale Trust
He carries me in his arms.

Jesus, thank you for meeting me in all my weariness and with all my burdens. I know you didn't intend for me to carry everything on my own. Help me remember that I can come to you no matter what and that you will take my load. Especially when my anxiety flares, help me remember that my joy, peace, and strength reside not in my own effort but in your faithful presence. Amen.

2

God's Help for the Engine in My Chest

God is our refuge and strength,
always ready to help in times of trouble.
—PSALM 46:1

I put my hand on my husband's heart. "It's like there is an engine in my chest. And it's revving, revving, revving for no reason. That's what this anxiety feels like." His look of confusion didn't really change.

"So even if my mind is fine, even if I'm not worried or stressed about anything in particular, the sensations in my body tell my mind that I'm *not* okay. The battle to keep calm and focused on what is true while the engine in my chest relentlessly spins . . . Well, it's exhausting."

I leaned my head on Chris's shoulder and tried to slow my breathing.

My husband and I don't speak the same emotional language. Mine has a lot of words; his, not so much. The language of mental health is also something I know well as someone living with clinical anxiety, but that's not Chris's world. Even though he loves me and wants to support me, it's hard for him to understand me.

I've tried countless ways of putting my anxiety into words. The anxiety doesn't always look or feel the same as worry or stress. It's not just trying to control a situation or fixating on a problem; it's a physiological experience. Like coffee jitters in my heart. Like the mental swirl of a dozen waking dreams that I can't escape. An outer calm masking an inner chaos.

That image of a car engine in my chest was God's grace—evidence of God's always-ready help in the middle of real-life struggle. While my husband still couldn't fully relate to my experience, this analogy provided a bridge of greater understanding.

If you struggle with anxiety, it's easy to question your feelings and try to keep them hidden. *Am I making all this up? Should I keep it to myself? Should I just try to ignore it and move on?*

The internal battle is real. But here's what I've learned: It's worth it to push through the pain, fear, and awkwardness to tell someone how you really feel. Why? There is power in bringing our struggles out of the darkness of isolation and into the light of shared experience.

When I refuse to hide, I open myself to the light. Shame can't live in the light. Fear doesn't grow in the light. So, I stand in my kitchen, resting my head on my husband's chest as morning light streams through smudged windows, and I know that God sees me. No inner darkness can hide me. His Word will guide me. He will guide you too.

> *Inhale Truth*
> God is my refuge and strength,
>
> *Exhale Trust*
> My ready help in trouble.

God, thank you for meeting me in the middle of my struggle. You are not far off. You are right here. May my anxiety cause me to run to you, my true safety and strength. Give me creative words and fresh courage to share my pain with others. I need your help. Every hour I need you. Amen.

3

Go to Bed and Take the B

It is useless for you to work so hard
from early morning until late at night,
anxiously working for food to eat;
for God gives rest to his loved ones.
—PSALM 127:2

I've been an achiever for as long as I can remember. When I was three, I was thrilled to master riding a bicycle before my older sister. When I was seven, I challenged my best friend Jack to a race to see who could climb to the tippy-top of a towering tree. In school, I took every advanced class, played three sports, joined multiple clubs, and was always in student government. Doing more and trying harder were how I felt safe, worthy, accepted.

One night in high school, as it was edging toward midnight, I was working to finish an essay. I sat in our upstairs landing in front of a clunky white Macintosh computer, feverishly typing. "Rebecca Dee!" my mom called up from the bottom of the stairs. "Are you still doing homework?" "Yeah, almost done," I lied. "It's late! Just go to bed and take the B!" she hollered.

Go to bed and settle for a B? Stop striving and accept less than the best? It was the most preposterous suggestion my adolescent ears had ever heard. Clearly perfectionism and a desire to perform had a hold on me!

I'm not sure when or how the belief took root—maybe out of my desire for control as a child of divorce or maybe as the youngest of three sisters, desperate to be noticed; whatever the reason, I believed *I am what I achieve.* It took me decades to understand the truth that I am God's

6

daughter—*that* is the most important thing about me. Regardless of what I do or how I perform, I am loved by God. Period. The same is true for *you*.

Part of my journey has been learning to reframe the way I see rest and productivity. Rest is not a hindrance to achievement, like my high school self adamantly believed; rest is a vital part of being productive. Without physical sleep and mental breaks, our anxiety will skyrocket and we simply cannot operate at our best. Even more, rest is essential to experiencing God, so much so that he made it one of the Ten Commandments.

Rest is an act of dependence. Rest tells God you trust him to work on your behalf. Rest makes space to quiet your noisy, anxious soul long enough to hear his voice. And surely his voice would say, "I love you more than any achievement or grade."

Inhale Truth
I don't have to strive for God's love.

Exhale Trust
I can just rest in him.

God, I'm so prone to finding my identity in what I accomplish rather than in you. I know working for love, acceptance, or significance only fosters more anxiety. Help me see productivity and rest the way you do so I can experience the peace that my soul craves. Thank you for loving me no matter what I do. Show me what it looks like to rest in your love today. I want to trust you more. Amen.

4

The Beauty of "And"

Here on earth you will have many trials and sorrows.
But take heart, because I have overcome the world.
—JOHN 16:33

We live in a broken world where things break. Cars, relationships, and dreams break. Same with bodies, hearts, and minds. But we don't have to walk through the brokenness alone. This is what I like to call the beauty of "and." In this world we will have trouble, *and* Jesus has overcome the world! We are broken and face all kinds of trials, *and* Jesus will make all things beautiful in his time.

Focusing on God's presence and continual work in my life has been especially helpful as I wrestle with mental illness. In fact, I've discovered that reframing the way I see living in the "and" has made all the difference! Here are some "and" statements that are true for me:

I am a woman with anxiety, *and* the joy of the Lord is my strength.
I am weighed down, *and* I am carried.
I am sorrowful, *and* I am full of peace.
My sadness swells, *and* I am secure no matter my emotions.
I am often overwhelmed, *and* I am never completely overcome.

The Bible is also full of beautiful "ands"! The disciples were scared of the storm, *and* Jesus was with them. Paul had a thorn in his flesh, *and* God's grace was sufficient. Jesus died on the cross, *and* he rose from the dead. In the middle of the mess is where we meet Jesus. In the tension of "and" is where we experience his grace.

As an anxiety warrior and advocate, here's what I know: You can suffer from mental illness *and* be a faithful follower of Jesus. You can trust fully in God *and* be at the end of your rope. You can read your Bible every day *and* still need medication.

Spend time today identifying the beautiful "ands" in your life. Choose one of these and make it your breath prayer throughout the day:

I am weak, *and* I have access to God's strength.
I am struggling, *and* I am not alone.
I have areas to grow in, *and* God will help me bear fruit.

Jesus came for the broken. That's me. That's you. He is so able and willing to hold all our jagged pieces and make something beautiful.

> *Inhale Truth*
> My trials weigh heavy.
>
> *Exhale Trust*
> And Jesus has overcome.

Jesus, thank you for being mindful of my trials and troubles. You see and understand what I'm going through. You meet me in my sorrows with your strength. Help me keep believing that anxiety is just one half of the beautiful "and" you have for my life. You're always writing my story, always overcoming my pain with your power. I'm so grateful. Amen.

5

Longing for Home

Don't let your hearts be troubled. Trust in God, and trust also in me.
There is more than enough room in my Father's home.
—JOHN 14:1–2

I grew up in the home my great-grandfather built. A home filled with the laughter of sisters scavenging through dress-up clothes and putting on plays. A home filled with music as we practiced our instruments and James Taylor crooned sweet tunes in the kitchen. A home filled with the smell of my mom's freshly baked bread and holiday pies.

Home was cloth napkins and vegetables from the garden. Home was boisterous card games and an open door for friends or exchange students who needed a place to land.

But home was also ground zero for strain, confusion, and heartbreak. Home was the place my dad left when I was nine. Home was where we never seemed to have as much as everyone around us. Home was often empty, leaving me to climb through a window when I forgot my key *again*. Home was the tension of joy and grief, belonging and abandonment, hope and shame.

When my parents divorced, they agreed that my mom, my two older sisters, and I would stay in our house . . . until I turned eighteen. As I was choosing a prom dress and studying for finals, my mom was dyeing the carpet emerald green to hide the stains. When the For Sale sign went up, it felt like a punch in the gut.

For years after that I lived with the ache of not having a home. Sure, I was never without a place to stash my stuff and lay my head, but that wasn't the same as feeling deeply rooted. The longing for stability ratcheted my anxiety.

Yet the ache of upheaval revealed a deeper truth: This world is not my home.

We live in a world full of brokenness and uncertainty. God understands our need for belonging and security; he knit those desires into our DNA. While earthly homes will inevitably fall short, Jesus invites us to lift our anxious hearts and trust him. *Don't let your hearts be troubled*, he says. God is preparing a forever home marked by comfort and love. A home that can never be sold. A home with always enough room.

In moments of anxiety, when life feels chaotic or uncertain, let this promise steady you. Pause, breathe deeply, and reflect on what home means to you. Stability? Comfort? Being known? Jesus provides all these and more. This world may be full of turmoil, but in him we are safe, rooted, and held.

> *Inhale Truth*
> God is worthy of my trust.
>
> *Exhale Trust*
> My home is in him.

Jesus, thank you for preparing a home where I will always belong. When anxiety stirs in my heart and life feels uncertain, remind me that my true security is in you. Help me trust your promises and rest in the knowledge that you are my unshakable foundation. Root me deeply in your love and guide me as I walk through the challenges of this world. Amen.

6

Keep Crying Out for Mercy

"Jesus, Son of David, have mercy on me!"
"Be quiet!" the people in front yelled at him.
But he only shouted louder, "Son of David, have mercy on me!"
—LUKE 18:38–39

A blind man sat begging on the side of the road. He obviously couldn't see what was happening, but he could hear it. A large crowd was passing by. There was much commotion. Something significant was taking place in front of his sightless eyes. So, he asked what was going on. "Jesus of Nazareth is going by," they said.

At this, the blind man stopped his mumbled begging and shouted to the one who had become famous for miracles. He no longer blindly pleaded for bread or money; he boldly cried out for what he really needed: *mercy.*

Yet what did those around him do? They shushed him. They had heard his begging day after day after day. They had become callous to his plight, dismissive of his humanity. Maybe they thought his cries would prevent them from hearing what Jesus was saying. Maybe they were worried that the dirty blind beggar would distract Jesus from the miracle *they* needed.

But where the crowd reacted with annoyance, Jesus responded with compassion.

Jesus stopped walking and ordered for the man to be brought to him. Jesus heard the person in need, and he was eager to draw near. When the man and the Messiah came face-to-face, Jesus asked, *"What do you want me to do for you?"*[1]

It's a simple question with a seemingly obvious answer for the one who lived in darkness. But Jesus asked because he wanted the man to give voice to his needs. Jesus asked this desperate soul to articulate his deepest desire as an act of faith. And it was that faith that saved him.

Jesus invites you to cry out, to name your affliction, and to ask for what you need. He is eager to call you out of the crowd and meet you with compassion.

> *Inhale Truth*
> Jesus, I need your healing.
>
> *Exhale Trust*
> Jesus, I receive your mercy.

Jesus, thank you that my persistent pleas are not a burden to you. You are not put off by my cries. You never put me down or cast me aside. Instead, you see my brokenness and invite me to come to you. Oh, how I need you, Jesus. Have mercy on me. What do I want you to do for me? Lord, I want [tell him your greatest need]. I receive your merciful answer. Heal me and make me free. Amen.

7

Don't Wait to Deserve It

God saved you by his grace when you believed.
And you can't take credit for this; it is a gift from God.
—EPHESIANS 2:8

For my fortieth birthday, I got gift cards for a massage and T.J. Maxx. I rarely splurge on myself, so the thought of being pampered and buying a new outfit thrilled me. But ten months later, those gift cards were still in my wallet. Why? It's not like I don't enjoy new clothes! It's not like I don't have knots in my neck aching to be worked out. So why hadn't I embraced the benefits of these generous gifts?

The truth was, I hadn't gone shopping or scheduled a massage because I felt like I had to earn it. Every time I considered the joy of perusing the racks of T.J. Maxx, I thought about the twenty pounds I wanted to lose. *Do you really want to go up a size? Just wait till you slim down,* I'd tell myself.

A similar "just wait" game continued regarding the massage. *Just wait till you finish that project or reach that milestone or overcome that hurdle.* In other words, *just wait till you deserve it.* But is a gift meant to be earned? No. A gift is simply meant to be received.

Getting tangled up in cultural expectations of beauty and misplaced notions of where my value lies is a picture of how we often treat our gifts from God. God has given us the gifts of his extravagant love, unconditional forgiveness, amazing grace, peace that surpasses understanding, relentless hope, boundless joy, and abundant strength. But . . . how often do you leave those gifts tucked in your Bible, hidden in your proverbial wallet, because you subconsciously feel like you have to do *more* before you embrace all God is offering *now*?

Scripture is super clear that God's gifts are by grace alone. There is no grace *plus*. No God's grace plus our effort. No grace plus grit or morality or smaller-sized jeans. We were never meant to work for God's love, forgiveness, or acceptance. We simply get to show up and receive. Show up anxious. Show up calm. Show up happy or sad. Show up fit or flabby. Our internal emotions and outward appearances don't disqualify us from the grace Jesus came to give. He simply invites us to show up acknowledging our sin and brokenness and desperate need for him.

When anxiety whispers that you need to do more or be better, remember that God's grace meets you right where you are. You don't have to be free of anxiety or have everything figured out to receive his love. Let go of the "just wait" mentality and embrace his gifts today.

Inhale Truth
God's grace is mine today.

Exhale Trust
I receive his beautiful gifts.

God, the gifts you give are so good. I could never earn them—and you don't ask me to. Thank you for simply inviting me to receive. Help me show up just as I am—anxious, broken, or weary—and trust that your grace is sufficient for me. Teach me to see myself the way you see me. I open my hands to everything you have for me. Amen.

PEACE
PRACTICE
1

Move

**Praise his name with *dancing*,
accompanied by tambourine and harp.**

—PSALM 149:3

When you move your body, something amazing happens: Your brain releases endorphins, those God-designed mood boosters that help melt away stress and lift your spirit. Physical activity also helps release muscle tension, a sneaky way anxiety tries to take up space in your body.

So if you're feeling overwhelmed or weighed down—move! Even when you don't *feel* like it.

Crank up the music and dance in your kitchen. Step outside for a walk and let fresh air fill your lungs. Shake out your arms, bounce with your knees, or do a few jumping jacks right where you are.

Your body is a gift from the Lord. Honor him by using it— and praising him with it!

8

Empathy Overload

> He heals the brokenhearted
> and bandages their wounds.
> —PSALM 147:3

One of my biggest anxiety triggers is what I call empathy overload. When someone I care about is struggling, I internalize it. This can happen even if I don't know the person! Watching the evening news, seeing a Go-FundMe page shared on Facebook, hearing about a tragedy in my community or a family in need—it's like my own heart begins to bleed. The reaction is even more intense when someone I personally know is facing hardship. I *feel* it all in my body. In my soul. Which often results in my anxiety taking on a life of its own.

Just last night I couldn't sleep. Again. I was feeling so deeply for a person I love who is going through severe heartache. This morning God reminded me of his truth: He alone is the one who can heal a broken heart. He alone holds the bandage our bleeding souls need. He is not a distant or uncaring God. He is the God who comes close, who bends low, who isn't afraid of our ugly trauma or open wounds.

One of my favorite names of God in the Bible is Jehovah-Rapha, "the Lord who heals." This is the name that appears in passages like Psalm 103:3, which tells us, "He forgives all my sins and heals all my diseases," and Isaiah 61:1 that declares, "The Spirit of the Sovereign LORD is upon me, for the LORD has anointed me to bring good news to the poor. He has sent me to comfort the brokenhearted and to proclaim that captives will be released and prisoners will be freed."

So, I remember again that Jehovah-Rapha is who my friend needs. My deep-feeling empathy is part of how God made me, but its purpose is not to ignite a spiral of anxiety. Rather, it's an invitation to pray for those who are hurting and in need of the Healer.

We cannot save anyone—ourselves included. But Jesus can. Let your deep concern, your empathy, and even your anxiety lead you to deeper trust in him. And if you're the one whose heart is shattered or spirit is bruised, call on Jehovah-Rapha and take heart knowing he is near.

> *Inhale Truth*
> Jehovah-Rapha
>
> *Exhale Trust*
> The Lord who heals is near.

God, thank you that it's not up to me to fix, save, or heal anyone. Yet my heart often aches for the brokenhearted. I know your heart aches too. Instead of allowing my empathy to transfer to anxiety, please use my tender heart to activate a powerful prayer life. Come near to those who are hurting today. I trust you. Amen.

9

You Belong to God, Not Fear

> God has not given us a spirit of fear and timidity,
> but of power, love, and self-discipline.
> —2 TIMOTHY 1:7

My anxiety loves to tell me that I'm incapable. Anxiety says, *The work is too much and the road ahead is too rocky, so you'd better just stay put. Stay stuck.* This voice gets louder every time I try to tackle something new or am on the cusp of a breakthrough. This voice tries to undermine growth and convince me that my anxiety is an immovable barrier so I might as well turn back (or just wallow in my overwhelm like a limp noodle left too long in boiling water).

This, my friend, is not the voice of God. But great news: We can learn to easily distinguish the dissonance of anxiety from the veracity of God's voice.

One key marker of anxiety is fear. Fear of failure. Fear of overwhelm. Fear of unknowns or disappointment or not being in control. But Scripture says that God has not given us a spirit of fear. What did God give instead? A spirit of power, love, and self-discipline.

God knows we are prone to be afraid! It's scary to step into a new situation. It's hard to overcome internal and external struggles, to allow God to stretch our faith and use the talents he gave us. But God is not limited by our fear, and he doesn't want us to live limited either.

Fear and anxiety are obnoxious cousins. But they're not your family. You, dear one, belong to God. And God gives his children only *good* gifts.

Your invitation today is to recognize the voice of anxiety and the spirit of fear in your life, and then respond with the power of God's Spirit instead. With him you can confidently take the next step forward.

> **Inhale Truth**
> Fear is not from God.
>
> **Exhale Trust**
> I have his power, love, and sound mind.

God, thank you that I don't have to stay stuck in my anxiety; I don't have to fear the road ahead because your Spirit goes with me. Indeed, your Spirit is in me. Help me exchange my feelings of hopelessness for the truth of your power. Reshape my belief that I'm unlovable with the truth of your deep love. And rewire my bent toward anxiety with the truth of your sound mind. Amen.

10

Stop Stuffing Grief in the Closet

The LORD is close to the brokenhearted;
he rescues those whose spirits are crushed.
—PSALM 34:18

Grief is a peculiar companion. It follows its own timeline, often sending emotional reminders long before significant dates arrive on the calendar. Every December, I feel a familiar ache in my chest. Tears threaten to spill over. I find myself snapping at my kids while they decorate ginger-bread houses with candy and icing. *What's wrong with me?* I wonder. And then it hits me: This is grief, another one of anxiety's cousins. Grief and anxiety can feel similar and intensify each other. I've tried to push these feelings away, but now I understand the power of making space for them.

It's tempting to think that life would be easier if we could just block out or avoid our pain. But acknowledging our grief is essential for moving through it. Ignoring it accomplishes nothing. I've tried that approach before, and it's like stuffing things you don't know how to deal with into a closet and hoping it won't burst open when company arrives. But just hiding grief doesn't make it disappear.

When I feel a lump in my throat or dull ache in my chest, I stop blaming myself and gently ask, *What or whom are you really sad about?* I create space to explore the answer. Whether you've lost a loved one, a dream, a relationship, your health, your home, or hope, you're likely carrying some form of grief. The real question is this: What will you do with it? Will you continue to lock it away in a dark closet, risking an explosion of emotions at an inopportune moment? Or will you acknowledge the pain that tugs at your heart and give it the attention it requires?

I know it's uncomfortable, but consider this: Denying our anxiety and grief ultimately means denying our need for a Savior.

Without Jesus, the pain of loss would feel everlasting. He entered this weary world to bear the weight of every sorrow we face. The prophet Isaiah foretold that Jesus would be "a man of sorrows, acquainted with deepest grief."[2] Because of this, we don't have to hide, stuff, or ignore our anguish. We can bring our grief and anxiety directly to the cross— and then gaze upon the empty tomb, knowing that Jesus understands and overcame it all.

> *Inhale Truth*
> God is close to my broken heart.
>
> *Exhale Trust*
> He will save me and heal me.

Lord, I'm grateful you understand my grief, my sorrow, my broken heart. You do not judge me when my anxiety flares or when I don't know how to process my feelings. Please show me how to welcome my grief so I can move through these overwhelming feelings and receive your healing. You know what I'm going through. Help me to see you here. Amen.

11

Jesus Will Come for You

**I cling to you;
your strong right hand holds me securely.
—PSALM 63:8**

I have a friend who was going through a difficult time. Difficult is actually an understatement. Her circumstances were brutal. Her mental, emotional, and physical health were suffering. She felt paralyzed by her situation and hopeless that it would change. She believed in God but felt far from him. Have you been in a place like that? Are you there today?

As I was praying for my friend, the Lord gave me a picture. I saw my friend in a dim room, crumpled on the floor. She was downcast, dejected, stuck. She wanted to get up, to run out of the room, but she couldn't. So Jesus came near. He entered her darkness, knelt beside her, and lifted her chin.

"See me," he said. "I am here with you. You don't have to do anything. I will carry you." Then Jesus picked her up. As soon as he did, a shaft of light appeared. Cradled like a child in his arms, she rested her head on his chest. And Jesus stepped into the light and carried her out of the dark.

This, my friend, is a picture for you too. Even when you've been abandoned or betrayed by others, even when you feel like a failure or feel stuck in the consequences of your own choices, even when the world has been unkind and your luck has been lousy and it feels like nothing—ever—seems to go your way, know this: Jesus will come for you.

You don't have to earn his love or prove you deserve his rescue. All you have to do is cling to him when he comes. Lift your eyes to Jesus as he lifts you up. Stop wondering whether he'll come or how long you must wait. The Rescuer is already there. Don't stay fixated on your pain or your shame. Look up! See the loving eyes of your compassionate God. He grieves over your wounds, and he's there with a heavenly first aid kit to mend your broken spirit and wrap your battered soul in the healing bandages of his love and grace.

Picture Jesus holding you. Picture yourself resting your head close to his heart. And watch him carry you into the light.

Inhale Truth
Jesus will come for me.

Exhale Trust
I cling to him now.

God, thank you for speaking through both Scripture and pictures. Please use my imagination to reveal deeper truths about you. Speak to my heart, Jesus. I need you to meet me in my anxiety, darkness, and despair. I need you to pick me up and carry me to healing and freedom. Rescue me, Jesus. I am yours. Amen.

12

A New Way of Thinking

> Don't copy the behavior and customs of this world, but let God
> transform you into a new person by changing the way you think.
> Then you will learn to know God's will for you,
> which is good and pleasing and perfect.
> —ROMANS 12:2

In countless remarkable ways, we are the by-products of our world. Sometimes our "world" is our small family of origin. I know how to create a beautiful fruit platter from years of watching my mom skillfully wash berries and slice melons. I inherited a passion for competitive card games from my dad along with the practice of putting peanut butter on my French toast. (Don't knock it till you try it.) I also inherited family patterns of trauma and dysfunction. You too?

The world at large is also a powerful influence in our lives. Take fear, for example. Did you know humans are born with only two innate fears? The fear of falling and the fear of loud noises.[3] Everything else is learned. We learn to be afraid of the size of our bodies and disappointing people. We learn to fear risk, failure, and public speaking. The world also teaches us how to deal with our fears—and that method is usually to ignore them and try harder!

The world's way of thinking tells us we've got to handle every hurdle on our own. Worldly wisdom argues that if we work hard enough (or even worry enough), we can mitigate risks, guarantee acceptance, and control future outcomes. Yet this thinking gets us only so far. Working hard to manage results, impress people, and keep ourselves safe might feel good in the moment. But thinking rooted in fear is ultimately self-focused. It's about getting what feels good to us—which discounts God's best.

Seeking our own security or trying to please others is garbage compared to the goodness God has for us! Paul makes it clear that to know God's good, pleasing, and perfect will, we each need to be transformed by God into a new person—*by changing the way we think*!

Take a moment today to consider this: In what ways does your life reflect the world more than it reflects Jesus? Ask God to reveal the fears or thought patterns driving those behaviors. Are you caught in people-pleasing? Overwhelmed by worry? Trying to control everything? Are you afraid of being rejected, abandoned, or unloved? Bring those things to God—and invite him to renew your mind with his truth.

Change your thinking by scrolling Instagram less and reading Scripture more. Create new patterns and neural pathways by turning off the news and turning up worship music. Spend less time consuming media and more time meditating on God's promises. We will never regret a life shaped by God.

> **Inhale Truth**
> I need less of this world
>
> **Exhale Trust**
> And more of Jesus.

God, please change the way I think. I recognize that my anxiety and fear increase when I'm rehashing my fears instead of rehearsing your truth. I don't want the world to be my model for safety or success. I want to know your will and honor you with my life. Show me what's holding me back. Transform me, Jesus. Thank you for always working for my best. I trust your good plans and faithful ways. Amen.

13

The Badge of Weariness

Those who trust in the LORD will find new strength.
They will soar high on wings like eagles.
They will run and not grow weary.
They will walk and not faint.
—ISAIAH 40:31

I am a woman well acquainted with weariness. I've known weariness in motherhood. (Hello, having three boys in three and a half years!) I've known weariness in work. (Hello, juggling multiple part-time jobs to meet the needs of my family.) I've known weariness in hard relationships, physical ailments, and mental illness. And I know I'm not alone.

I've noticed in myself and others two primary responses to weariness. The first is wearing weariness like a badge of honor. This posture says, *Look at me! Look at all the stuff I'm doing. Look at how hard my life is. Give me a pat on the back and five gold stars for being a self-sacrificing martyr.*

The second response is to wear weariness like a badge of shame. This posture says, *Don't look at me. Why is this so hard? Why can everyone else hold it all together while I'm falling apart? I'm doomed to failure. No one understands what I'm going through or is able to help.*

The fundamental problem with both of these coping strategies is that they put all the focus on ourselves. Both the badge of honor and the badge of shame cause us to turn inward and cling to either false confidence or false defeat. Anytime we're living in cycles of falsehood, our souls will surely feel the effects.

The truth is, our weariness isn't something to overcome in grin-and-bear-it pride, nor is it something to shrink under in self-defeating shame. Our weariness is an indication of how much we need God's strength. It's an invitation to trust the God who parted the Red Sea for overwhelmed refugees, the God who empowered a young shepherd to defeat a giant warrior with a mere stone and sling, the God who fed a hungry crowd of thousands with a young boy's little lunch. Yes, this is our God!

God doesn't need your strength. His is more than enough! But he does require your trust. Offer your weariness and anxiety to Jesus and receive his strength in return.

Inhale Truth
I lay down my badge of weariness.

Exhale Trust
In God I find new strength.

Lord, you know why I am weary. You know every anxious thought in my head, discouragement in my heart, and exhausted bone in my body. Help me see my weariness the way you do. Show me how to give it to you and receive your strength instead. I'm desperate for you. Help me trust you. Amen.

14

The Bigger Picture of Anxiety

Sing for joy, O heavens!
Rejoice, O earth!
Burst into song, O mountains!
For the LORD has comforted his people
and will have compassion on them in their suffering.
—ISAIAH 49:13

Anxiety is often more than a list of worries and woes that need to be prayed over or surrendered to the Lord (especially for those of us with clinical anxiety). Is it helpful and wise to pray? Absolutely! The Bible says, "Never stop praying."[4] And of course, we should give our worries and fears to God. I believe wholeheartedly that a surrendered life is an abundant life.

But along with beating the drum of trust and surrender, I will continue to clang the cymbal that declares anxiety is not always synonymous with fear-driven worry. Anxiety can also be a mental health disorder with a host of symptoms. As I've shared, my anxiety disorder can manifest in a racing mind, extreme sadness, heightened irritability, trouble concentrating, and difficulty breathing, as well as in being overwhelmed by tasks or stimuli I'm typically able to handle.

I'm no doctor or psychologist, so I'll leave the diagnosing to the professionals, but here is one simple litmus test that's been helpful for me when it comes to differentiating between common stress and a more serious level of anxiety: Evaluate the persistency and severity. As in, how persistent or severe are your symptoms or experience?

Let's use a rash as an example. Everyone is bound to deal with some form of bumps, itch, or skin discomfort from time to time. These things usually resolve on their own or with simple self-care or home remedies. Other times, however, the itching might become so severe or the pain so intense that it distracts you at work or keeps you up at night. Or maybe the rash spreads or lasts longer than a month. These are signs that it's time for outside intervention. The same is true for anxiety. If your anxiety is severe or persistent, don't hesitate to get help.

God cares about your whole person—body, soul, *and* mind. The brokenness of this world was never God's design. Yet he is so faithful to meet us in it. He showers us with his love and compassion. He offers us his strength to face another day. Healing may come while there is still earthly oxygen in our lungs. But even if it does not, healing will come.

Inhale Truth
God cares for my suffering.

Exhale Trust
His comfort sustains me.

Lord, I will praise you when I'm doing well, and I will praise you when I'm suffering. You are always worthy of my praise because you are the same yesterday, today, and forever. Please help me understand my anxiety. I don't want to hide in my struggles—and I especially don't want to hide from you. Thank you for having compassion on your people. Open my heart to receive help in any form you want to give it. Amen.

PEACE
PRACTICE
2

Connect

Two people are better off than one, for they can *help each other* succeed. If one person falls, the other can reach out and help. But someone who falls alone is in real trouble.

—ECCLESIASTES 4:9–10

Anxiety thrives in isolation, but you don't have to face it by yourself. Staying connected is vital for your mental and emotional well-being.

I know it can feel like you're carrying your struggle all by yourself—but you're not. That heaviness? You don't have to hold it alone. There *is* someone who cares—someone who's willing to listen, offer encouragement, or just be present with you in the hard. When you take the brave step to reach out, it's a gentle reminder that you belong. And that reminder? It can make the weight of worry and loneliness feel a little lighter.

So send a quick text asking for prayer. Show up at church, even if it feels easier to stay home. Let a friend in on how you're really doing and ask for help.

God created us to need each other. Be brave and let yourself be known.

15

Stupid Mistakes and God's Perfect Love

I am convinced that nothing can ever separate us from God's love.
—ROMANS 8:38

Mistakes are one of life's greatest teachers. Now, that sounds like a great quote to plaster on a puppy-clad poster in an elementary classroom— but it's not a pleasant truth to live out.

Recently I messed up. I was talking on the phone while driving to an office I'd never been to before, and I missed a turn. I didn't realize my error until it was too late. By the time I turned around, backtracked, and made it to my appointment, I was told that the doctor could no longer see me. I had waited months for this appointment, taken time away from work, and arranged childcare . . . and now I had to reschedule.

I stood in front of the receptionist with anxiety crawling up my neck. I felt flustered and sweaty and desperate to turn back time. I reluctantly accepted the new appointment card and walked away with my head down. I drove home, silently wiping tears of frustration and berating myself for my mistake.

My reaction was less about driving distracted and suffering the consequence and more about my secret belief that I simply shouldn't make mistakes. I often held myself to an impossible standard, putting focus and efficiency on a pedestal. I believed that messing up meant there was something fundamentally wrong with me.

But here's the truth: Perfectionism is a myth. Performance-based living is anxiety inducing and soul crushing. So why do we live like a mistake-free existence is the ultimate achievement?

The goodness of God is that he loves us *always*—not just on the days when we have our ducks in a row and everything goes as planned. We are no less valued when we mess up.

When we view our mistakes through the truth of God's Word and his unshakable, never-ending love, everything changes. Our missteps and mistakes don't disqualify us from God's blessings. (He knows we're imperfect, prone to distraction and wrong turns!) As long as we keep returning to the unfailing road map of Scripture, God will lovingly guide us back to the gift of his grace and purpose for our lives. Let that truth ease your anxious soul.

Inhale Truth
Making mistakes is human.

Exhale Trust
I am secure in God's love.

Jesus, I'm so grateful that you are perfect and I don't have to be. Yet I get anxious and knotted up when I get something wrong. Please help me make wise choices that honor you and others, and receive your grace when I don't. Thank you that no mistake can separate me from your love. I choose to keep turning back to you. Amen.

16

The First Step Toward Freedom

God is our merciful Father and the source of all comfort. He comforts us in all our troubles so that we can comfort others.
—2 CORINTHIANS 1:3–4

Anxiety manifests differently for everyone. For me, it often feels like a deep physical and emotional pressure in my chest, making it hard to catch my breath. It's an unending well of sadness that doesn't match my circumstances. And for a long time, I felt like it was my fault.

I believed that if I just prayed harder or got more sleep, I could get over it. I thought that if I simply stopped procrastinating, took extra vitamins, and trusted God more, then I could fix myself. Daily prayer and adequate rest are absolutely important! But what I failed to understand was that my symptoms were a legitimate indication that something was off-kilter. My spinning thoughts and heightened irritability didn't mean my faith was weak; they were like flashing neon signs signaling I needed help.

I ignored those signs for a long time.

When all my attempts to climb out of my dark hole failed, I remembered a friend had once told me she took anxiety medication. At the time, I honestly thought that anxiety was just being overly worried and that someone could simply stop. But now I wondered whether I had gotten it all wrong.

So, I called my friend. Even though it had been a long time since we connected . . . even though I worried I would choke on my words and that she wouldn't understand . . . I reached out anyway and told her what I was going through. She listened patiently and responded with compassion. She didn't try to fix my feelings. She told me that it sounded like there was more going on than ordinary stress. Shortly thereafter I started going to counseling—one of the most transformative decisions I ever made.

Giving voice to the struggle is the first step toward healing.

I'm so thankful my friend was willing to bravely share about her anxiety all those years ago. Though I didn't relate to her feelings at the time, God used the echo of her voice when I needed it most. Her honesty told me I wasn't alone and that anxiety wasn't a life sentence.

If your present trouble is a source of shame, try reframing it as an opportunity to receive God's comfort. Then pass that comfort on to someone else. You have no idea how your story might be the spark of hope they need.

Inhale Truth
God's comfort is with me.

Exhale Trust
I will not suffer alone.

God, thank you for being my merciful Father and the source of all comfort. Oh, how I need you. It's tempting to feel like what I'm going through today is what I'll be dealing with forever. Give me hope to believe that you're still writing my story and that I won't always feel this way. Provide the strength I need to honestly share my struggles. Provide someone trustworthy to listen. Thank you that I am never alone and that healing is coming. Amen.

17

Expectations vs. Expectancy

Listen to my voice in the morning, LORD.
Each morning I bring my requests to you and wait expectantly.
—PSALM 5:3

We carry expectations like we carry our phones—without even thinking about it. We expect the meeting to go smoothly, the shirt we ordered online to fit just right, and maybe, just maybe, our kids to stop complaining and finally listen. Some expectations are small and passing. Others run deep and leave us aching when they go unmet.

And it's not just the everyday stuff. Especially at the start of a new year, I've got fitness goals and business benchmarks I want to hit. I'm chasing big dreams while trying to hold on to small, meaningful habits. I have expectations for my marriage, my kids, my houseplants, and even the nagging pain in my elbow that I'm hoping will just go away.

Whether you're thinking about your family, job, education, retirement, relationships, health, or dreams, it's natural to wonder about what's to come. It's not bad to desire and hope for good things. But often, our expectations are rooted in our own abilities or others' actions. Will I have what it takes to make my goal happen? Will that person come through and do the thing I want or need them to do? Here's the problem we face: Gripping too tightly to our expectations sets us up for disappointment. Disappointment increases anxiety and limits our ability to see God move.

So how do we handle our hopes and fears, desires and needs that all pile into a mountain of expectations? We talk to God! We follow the countless examples in Scripture and pour out our hearts to him. Talking to

God is an incredible privilege of being his children. Attentive listening is a beautiful part of who God is as our heavenly Father.

But sometimes we need to reframe the way we talk to God. Instead of coming to him with your expectations, what if you approached God with expectancy? What if you stopped focusing on what *you* want to happen and start focusing on what *God* will make happen?

Expectations, when unmet, can easily lead to discouragement and anxiety. But expectancy opens the door of your heart for deeper curiosity, trust, and faith to take root. Talk openly with the Lord today. Write down your greatest needs—and then choose a posture of expectancy as you wait for him to answer.

> *Inhale Truth*
> God listens when I speak.
>
> *Exhale Trust*
> I trust and wait expectantly.

Lord, thank you for being the God who hears and responds. I recognize that my expectations are limited by my own knowledge, perspective, and agenda—even by my anxiety. But you, Lord, are so much kinder, wiser, and more faithful than I could ask or think. I give you my expectations and choose a posture of expectancy. I can't wait to see what you do. Amen.

18

Rethinking Our Thorns

My grace is all you need. My power works best in weakness.
—2 CORINTHIANS 12:9

It's taken me a long time to learn one of life's most important lessons: My limitations don't disqualify me from God's goodness.

We all have limited resources and limited energy, and please tell me I'm not the only one who feels like patience is in short supply. Our limitations can feel crippling, like lead blankets on our shoulders or shackles around our ankles, weighing us down and preventing us from living the lives we desire. We live in a self-sufficient culture that says we should be it all, do it all, and have it all. Falling short is not an option.

But God's Word tells a different story.

In 2 Corinthians 12, the apostle Paul talks about having what he called a thorn in his flesh. We don't know the specifics, but certainly it was a limitation, a hardship, something he desperately wished he could change. Paul prayed three times for God to take this thorn away. God answered, "My grace is sufficient for you, for my power is perfected in weakness."[5]

God didn't change Paul's circumstance. Instead, God offered his power. That is what he wants to do in your life today too! Your limitation—whatever makes you feel like you'll never be or do or have enough—is actually the doorway to experiencing more of God's power and provision in your life.

I know, because he's done it for me.

One of the biggest limitations in my life has been my struggle with anxiety and depression. When the uncontrollable tears come, when exhaustion runs bone-deep but I can't sleep, when my sensitivity is high and irritability through the roof, I feel doomed to defeat. Like Paul, I've begged God to take this thorn away. And up to this point, his loving answer has been, *I will use your pain and struggle for my good purposes. I would rather you limp toward me than run off in your own strength.*

It's time to reframe the way you look at your limitations. Weakness is not a detriment—it's an opportunity to receive God's abundant grace and strength.

Inhale Truth
God's grace is all I need.

Exhale Trust
My weakness for his strength.

God, thank you that your grace is exactly what I need—you are more than sufficient for every trial and challenge I face. Please help me see my limitations as an opportunity to experience your power—not just in theory but in lived experience. I need your real strength for my real life. Help me receive everything you want to give me today. Amen.

19

Desperate to Understand

The LORD grants wisdom!
From his mouth come knowledge and understanding.
—PROVERBS 2:6

I found myself sitting in my therapist's office again. For a year and a half I had been in a really good place, but now my anxiety and depression were making a comeback. I needed help.

As I shifted on the sofa and hugged a pillow, I felt grateful for my therapist, who had become a trusted companion on my mental health journey. Even so, discussing the hidden struggles that plague me is never easy. I fumbled through describing the physical symptoms I had been experiencing. The pulsing bursts of adrenaline that gave way to a sudden drain, leaving me completely exhausted. After just a few hours of work each day, my energy fizzled out and I would crash. As someone who has always been able to push through anxiety and fatigue for the sake of productivity and pleasing others, it was unsettling to face a forced shutdown.

My therapist listened attentively and explained that it sounded like I was operating outside my "window of tolerance." Unfamiliar with the term, I listened as she elaborated. Each of us has a window of tolerance where our parasympathetic nervous system functions optimally, allowing us to feel peaceful and grounded while managing stress. However, both external circumstances and internal imbalances can move us outside this window.

If you are bumped above your window, you enter *hyperarousal* and can experience a racing heart and other physical anxiety symptoms. Conversely, if you bump below your window, it leads to *hypoarousal,* where your nervous system becomes overloaded and responds with depressive symptoms, essentially telling your body to shut down.[6] These terms described my situation perfectly. I was volleying between operating above and below my window of tolerance, and I desperately needed to get back within the window.

Receiving a framework to understand what was happening inside me was a tremendous gift and one of the most empowering and healing aspects of therapy for me. I've come to realize that while anxiety and depression are part of my genetic makeup, they don't have to define me. I don't have to suffer alone or stay stuck, and neither do you.

Inhale Truth
God leads me to understanding.

Exhale Trust
With him I can face anything.

God, thank you for good therapists, doctors, pastors, teachers, mentors, and friends. I know what it's like to feel stuck, to need healing, and to not know how to get it. Please help me pay attention to what's happening in me and around me, and lead me to the help I need. Guide me in your wisdom and truth. What do you want me to know? I'm listening. Amen.

20

When You're at the End of Your Rope

"I have had enough, LORD," he said.
—1 KINGS 19:4

As my therapist and I talked more about what causes me to hover outside my window of tolerance and how I can get back to center, she repeatedly used the word *nurture*. "Becky, what would it look like to nurture yourself?" When I hear that word, I think about the way a mother cuddles a young child or the way a gardener tends to fledgling plants. Nurturing myself has never been part of my push-through vocabulary or mentality. I told my counselor I would ponder it.

A few weeks later, I came upon the story of when Elijah reached the end of his rope. The circumstances that got him to that point are fascinating and worth reading. But it was the scene that unfolds in 1 Kings 19 that really got me. "I have had enough, LORD," Elijah cried out. The prophet, who had seen God's goodness and power and faithfulness again and again, was done. So done in fact that he was ready to just die. The story continues:

> Then he lay down and slept under the broom tree. But as he was sleeping, an angel touched him and told him, "Get up and eat!" He looked around and there beside his head was some bread baked on hot stones and a jar of water! So he ate and drank and lay down again.
>
> Then the angel of the LORD came again and touched him and said, "Get up and eat some more, or the journey ahead will be too much for you." (verses 5–7)

There are times to push through, and there are times to rest. This scripture shows us that when we just can't keep going, when we're too tired or discouraged or anxious, when something inside us is waving the white flag and crying out "Too much!"—God will take care of us. He will nurture us.

God didn't send an angel to give Elijah a pep talk or to chastise him about his lack of faith or endurance. No. God let Elijah sleep. Then he sent an angel to give him something to eat and drink. Repeat.

If your body or mind has had enough, maybe it's time to stop pushing through and simply rest. Maybe it's time to think about what it looks like to nurture yourself. Talk to God about how you're feeling. Consider also sharing with a trusted friend, mentor, or counselor. Your mental and physical health are important to God. He loves you and is eager to take care of you.

Inhale Truth
God hears my cry.

Exhale Trust
He will take care of me.

God, thank you for caring about Elijah and about me. Thank you for being tender and compassionate when I am at the end of my rope. Thank you that what feels like a dead end to me is just the beginning of your care and compassion. How do you want to nurture me today? What does it look like to receive your provision and love? Show me, Lord. Amen.

21

The Real Purpose of Fear

Don't be afraid, for I am with you.
Don't be discouraged, for I am your God.
I will strengthen you and help you.
I will hold you up with my victorious right hand.
—ISAIAH 41:10

Fear gripped me as a child. I was afraid of being kidnapped walking home from school. I was afraid of robbers breaking in to my house. I would imagine elaborate scenarios and plan out exactly what I would do and where I would hide. Over the years I've also been afraid of snakes, my children getting hurt, making a wrong decision, waking up with new pimples, driving to new places, disappointing people, and having too much to do and not enough time to do it.

Fear is a familiar companion for most of us. Fear says you're not safe. Fear says you're not in control. Fear says something bad is about to happen. And fear drives us to grip the steering wheels of our lives and drive as fast as we can away from discomfort. "Driving away" can look like numbing out, trying harder, building walls, or wallowing in worry.

But fear, like any emotion, is a gift from God. (Yes, our emotions are gifts!) Biologically, fear has a purpose: to alert us to danger. For example, fear is our nervous system's way of sounding the alarm—like when we hear footsteps behind us in a dark alley.

However, as an impact of living in a broken world, we often misinterpret the fear signal. We take any sign of fear as a green light to self-protect. And self-protection takes all kinds of forms. Pride is self-protection. Being critical of others is self-protection. Playing it safe, avoiding good risks, engaging in addictive behaviors, scrolling mindlessly, and prioritizing our comfort over obedience to God are all forms of self-protection. The more we self-protect, the more our lives are rooted in fear.

So what are we to do with our fear? Instead of a trigger for self-protection, God intended fear to be like an arrow pointing us back to our need for him. Over and over in Scripture, God commands us to not be afraid. But do you know what comes along with that command? The assurance of God's presence. Do you see the beauty? The gift? God isn't saying, *Fix yourself.* He's saying, *Fix your eyes on me.*

When we fixate on our circumstances and our ability (or lack thereof) to control them, fear will always rise. But when we focus on the promise of God's relentless presence, we remember that we don't have to be in control, because God is.

Let fear serve its best purpose: to remind you that God is always, always with you.

> *Inhale Truth*
> God's presence is with me.
>
> *Exhale Trust*
> He is greater than my fear.

God, thank you for the assurance of your presence, the truth of your fierce withness. When fear grips me, remind me to cling tightly to you. In the midst of my anxiety, remind me that you are always with me. Grant me a greater awareness of how near you are. Amen.

PEACE
PRACTICE
3

Journal

I still dare to hope
when I *remember* this:
The faithful love of the Lord never ends!
His mercies never cease.

—LAMENTATIONS 3:21–22

Journaling is like giving your mind permission to breathe. When you spill your swirling anxious thoughts onto paper, they lose some of their power, making room for clarity and peace. What once felt overwhelming starts to feel a little lighter.

And here's the beautiful part—when you look back and read old journals, you'll see how far you've come. Your own words will remind you of God's faithfulness, proof that even in the middle of the struggle, growth is happening.

It doesn't have to be fancy. Just grab a notebook, set a timer for five minutes, and pour your heart onto the page.

God is already there, ready to meet you with his faithful love.

22

The Ultimate Invitation

When God our Savior revealed his kindness and love,
he saved us, not because of the righteous things we had done,
but because of his mercy.
—TITUS 3:4–5

Friend, nothing in this book truly matters if you haven't surrendered your whole life to Jesus. Maybe you believe in God. Maybe you attend church on Christmas and Easter. Perhaps you picked up this book because anxiety has been holding you hostage and you're desperate for relief. Maybe you've tried therapy and medication, yoga and clean eating, but that deep, unsettled discontentment remains. You are tired of anxiety being the main character in your story. You don't want to spend the rest of your life striving, weary, and wondering whether you have to do it all alone.

Here's the most beautiful news: The end of our rope is where we discover the beginning of God's grace.

You were never meant to fix yourself or untangle your anxious soul alone. Trust me, I've tried! I've tried to erase my own shame, prove my worth, and earn others' approval. But the more I tried, the more tangled in anxiety I became. We all have made mistakes and carry regrets . . . *but God*.

"But God showed his great love for us by sending Christ to die for us while we were still sinners."[7]

God's love comes with an invitation: to acknowledge our brokenness and receive the gift of Jesus's sacrifice. Christ's death on the cross covers all our failures. His life is the payment that wipes our record clean. His victory over death paves the way for us to live with great hope and joy. And if you've already said yes to Jesus, be encouraged all over again that the God who came to earth to live and die for you is the same one who is with you in your anxiety.

Dear one, you are invited into God's kingdom—not a kingdom of rules and religious performance but one of love, peace, and true belonging. If you're tired of trying to be "good enough" and you believe Jesus died for your sins, you can accept his invitation of forgiveness and full life today! If your heart is pounding as you read this, that's God's Spirit stirring in you. The best way to move through your anxiety into lasting peace is to start a relationship with Jesus—or return to him if you've gone your own way.

Belonging to Jesus is the greatest gift we could ever receive.

Inhale Truth
I am saved by God's mercy and love.

Exhale Trust
I believe in Jesus.

Dear God, I've messed up and missed the mark. Please forgive me. I understand that I can't earn your love by trying hard or being a good person. Your love is a free gift. I accept that Jesus sacrificed his life for my sins. Please come into my heart. I don't want to do life by my own strength. I want to follow you. Amen.

23

Could Your Anxiety Be a Gift?

You intended to harm me, but God intended it all for good.
—GENESIS 50:20

In many ways, my anxiety has been a gift. (I never thought I'd say that!) When I'm in the throes of an anxiety attack, it doesn't *feel* like a gift at all. The same is true for so many of the trials we face: chronic illness, divorce, unemployment, natural disasters, or relational heartbreak. These hardships aren't made good simply because we search for silver linings.

Trying to tie up our hard stories with happy bows can actually hurt more than help. Maybe you've felt the sting of well-meaning but trite words meant to comfort you in your pain. Let's be clear: The brokenness we experience in our bodies, minds, and relationships was never God's plan. He doesn't delight in our suffering. But he is faithful to use it!

I never would've chosen to write anxiety into my story. I didn't imagine I'd be the woman crying in my car for no clear reason. Easily overwhelmed by too many lights or sounds. Tired but somehow still awake at 2 A.M. *But God.* (Those are two of the most powerful words we can cling to!)

But God takes what the enemy meant for evil and uses it for good. We see this so clearly in the story of Joseph. Sold into slavery by his own brothers, falsely accused, and imprisoned—Joseph's life was riddled with pain. Yet God worked through those years of hardship. Joseph rose to a position of power in Egypt, saving countless lives during a famine. And when he stood face-to-face with the brothers who betrayed him,

Joseph said, "You intended to harm me, but God intended it all for good" (Genesis 50:20).

This is the promise we hold on to: "In all things God works for the good of those who love him."[8] *All things.* My anxiety is where I've met God in some of the most tender, transformative ways. Through my anxiety God has equipped me to encourage and care for others. God is working in my life, and he's working in yours.

Is it okay to pray for healing and relief? Absolutely. Cry out to God in your thorns and storms. When he chooses to heal, we praise him. But if he doesn't deliver you on this side of heaven, praise him still—because his love and power are at work in your life either way.

Whatever you're facing today, know this: God is not finished with your story. Even in the midst of brokenness, he's weaving his goodness and purpose into your life. Trust him. He is faithful.

> *Inhale Truth*
> God works in all things.
>
> *Exhale Trust*
> He'll use my pain for good.

God, I'm so grateful you are in control of my life, even when it feels like all the odds are stacked against me. You are always for me, always with me, always working for my good. Help me trust you with today's difficulties and believe you can use them for tomorrow's blessings. Please transform my anxiety into a gift for me and others. Amen.

24

Wisdom for Every Need

If you need wisdom, ask our generous God, and he will give it to you.
He will not rebuke you for asking.
—JAMES 1:5

As a child, I could often be found with cuts and scrapes from running through rosebushes or racing the wind on my Rollerblades. Those bright red marks didn't bother me. Though inner fear sometimes plagued me, I reveled in outer toughness. So when I began complaining about frequent backaches, my mom sensed there was something real going on.

We tried stretching, heating pads, and warm baths, but the pain persisted. Medical examinations revealed no injuries or abnormalities. So what was happening?

Eventually, a doctor shifted the focus from a physiological explanation to my mental and emotional well-being. Was there any stress at home? The answer was yes. My parents had recently separated, and my dad moved out. The mystery of my pain was now becoming clear: My body was reacting physically to emotional stress. I was literally storing anxiety in my body.

As an adult, I can look back and see how my anxiety presented itself in ways we didn't recognize at the time. I never spoke about my racing thoughts or the sensation of being outside my body. I didn't realize that my occasional paralysis over schoolwork (when I normally thrived academically) was anxiety rearing its head.

As parents, grandparents, teachers, coaches, aunts, mentors, and friends, we have the privilege and responsibility to pay attention. We don't need to be trained mental health professionals to sense when a child or even a friend is struggling; we just need to be observant and ask God for wisdom to respond appropriately.

My mom couldn't see how the turmoil inside my mind was affecting my body. In a similar way, I've looked into my own anxious child's eyes and felt helpless. I've wiped away tears, witnessed tantrums, and listened to fears and sadness from a kid who feels misunderstood.

In these moments, I remind myself of the truth: Jesus sees, understands, and holds it all. If a child you know is struggling, listen to them, believe them, and ask God for guidance. That may mean seeking help from a doctor or therapist or simply being present and supportive.

You don't need to have all the answers—you just have to be willing to ask the Lord for wisdom and show up with love. God delights in giving both.

> *Inhale Truth*
> I ask God for wisdom.
>
> *Exhale Trust*
> He is generous to give it.

Lord, thank you for giving wisdom generously to all who ask for it. I'm here asking. Oh, how I need the insight and clarity that only you can give. It can be so hard to understand and untangle the stress, anxiety, and overwhelm I feel and sense in others. Grant me wisdom to know how to love and support those who are struggling—even if that person is me. Amen.

25

Jesus Comes Near

> I can never escape from your Spirit!
> I can never get away from your presence! . . .
> Your hand will guide me,
> and your strength will support me.
> —PSALM 139:7, 10

One of my favorite things about God is that he comes near. David told us the Lord is close to the brokenhearted. Isaiah said that God is like a shepherd who carries us close to his heart. God assured Moses and Joshua that he was with them and would never leave them. The Lord met Daniel in the lions' den and Shadrach, Meshach, and Abednego in the furnace. Jesus came near to the woman caught in adultery, the woman who bled, Peter's mother-in-law who was sick, and every afflicted person he met.[9]

This is our God. I have felt God's nearness in the throes of anxiety and when hot tears of despair have stained my red cheeks. I've known his nearness while tending to a feverish child and when looking at a checking account without enough dollars. God comes near not because we have it all together but because he knows how desperately we need him.

And here's what's so beautiful: He meets us even when we don't perceive his presence.

After Jesus's death and resurrection, two of his followers were traveling to Emmaus. Luke recorded, "Jesus himself came near and began to walk along with them."[10] God kept them from recognizing Jesus, likely to illustrate their spiritual blindness, but later they admitted that their hearts burned within them during the encounter.

I can relate to missing Jesus in the moment. You too? We get text messages from friends with the exact words we needed to hear and praise their intuition. We struggle to pay bills and somehow pick up extra work or receive gifts in the mail that cover the cost, then deem it our hard work or another's generosity. We long for clarity or direction, and when it comes, we give credit to the good advice we received or the merits of our own logic.

But what if every blessing, every comfort, and every encouragement are actually the manifestations of God's presence?

Wherever you are today and whatever is going on in your life, embrace the reality that Jesus comes near. Ask God to open the eyes of your heart so you can recognize his presence. Then lean in. Give thanks. He's right there with you.

> ### Inhale Truth
> God is always near.
>
> ### Exhale Trust
> He is my support and strength.

Lord, thank you for being the God who comes near. I wish I could walk with you down an actual road and hear your audible voice, but I'm grateful that your Spirit is in me and your presence is all around me. When I feel alone, afraid, anxious, or overwhelmed, help me recognize that you're right here with me. Amen.

26

Worth the Wait

What's important is that God makes the seed grow.
—1 CORINTHIANS 3:7

A green print hanging on my bathroom wall reads, "The day you plant the seed is not the day you eat the fruit." My friend Aliza hand-lettered it, and though it doesn't perfectly match the space, I hung it there as a daily reminder: Growth takes time, and that's okay.

We live in a world of hurry-up. I'll admit it—I don't like to wait. I don't like to wait in line at the grocery store or wait for my Amazon order. I don't like to wait for another episode of my favorite TV show, for an injury to heal, or for a dream to come to fruition. And I certainly don't like to wait for growth. Waiting feels like wasted time. But waiting is where growth happens.

So often I plant seeds in the soil of my life and impatiently expect instant fruit. I decide to fast from sugar, then foolishly hope that a week of self-control will erase months of unhealthy choices. Or I commit to being more patient with my kids and feel defeated when our home isn't magically peaceful overnight. The frustration feels heavy and like I'm failing before I've even begun.

When I convince myself that my life must produce instant results, anxiety starts to whisper. It starts to speak louder when I interpret a lack of fruit as failure—it says I'm not doing enough, that I'm not enough. But growth is not about proving myself; it's about trusting the process God designed.

The day you plant the seed is not the day you eat the fruit. Each day these words calm my anxious, hurry-up heart. When I savor a sweet strawberry or a juicy piece of watermelon, I'm reminded that every bit of good fruit takes time. God's work in me is no different—it's slow, deliberate, and always worth the wait.

Today, let the miracle of small seeds becoming delicious fruit remind you to trust the God who designed slow growth for your good. Take a moment to thank him for the work he's doing in you, even if you can't see the fruit just yet. Trust that his timing is perfect.

> *Inhale Truth*
> I don't have to hurry up.
>
> *Exhale Trust*
> God's growth is right on time.

God, thank you for the way you designed tiny seeds to be planted in the ground, hidden in dark soil, and steadily nourished by water and sunshine to eventually produce beautiful fruit. I trust this process with an orange or tomato, but help me trust this process in my own life. When I feel anxious in the waiting, remind me that you are the Master Gardener. Please cultivate patience and good fruit in me. Amen.

27

Receive the Rest You Need

Only in returning to me
and resting in me will you be saved.
In quietness and confidence is your strength.
—ISAIAH 30:15

A few years ago, I sensed the Lord calling me into a season of rest. That sounded lovely—peaceful even—but living it out was anything but easy. Slowing down stirred up all kinds of fear. What if I fell behind? What if I let someone down? My mind buzzed with anxiety, insisting I had to keep moving, keep producing, keep proving my worth. Rest felt like surrendering control . . . and honestly, I wasn't sure I knew how.

As I wrestled with God over what rest should look like and how I didn't have time for it, he impressed this truth firmly on my heart: *You're on the edge of burnout and breakdown, and I'm trying to save you.* Years of sleepless nights with three little ones blurred into the relentless rhythm of graduate school—all while still being fully present as a mom. And just when I thought I might catch my breath, one demanding work project after another piled on. There was no margin, no pause. I had been living in overdrive for far too long.

And then the Lord said, *Stop.*

When you're used to running full speed, stopping feels unnatural—maybe even impossible. I had to *learn* how to rest. What at first felt like losing control slowly revealed itself as vital for my mental health, my relationships, and the dreams God had placed in me.

In the past, I would pat myself on the back for unplugging for a long weekend, expecting that a short break would completely recharge me. I'd return from retreats or vacations still feeling weary but convince myself I should feel refreshed—and then wonder what was wrong with me when I didn't.

My season of intentional rest stretched into a full year. Looking back, I marvel at how God gently pruned my need to *do* and instead cultivated deeper trust and surrender as I learned to just *be*. Over the months, my soul softened. Weariness gave way to quiet strength, and new energy and creativity began to sprout in places I thought were barren.

God's call to rest isn't just about restoring our energy—it's about freeing us from the grip of anxiety and teaching us to trust him instead of our own efforts. Is God inviting you to lean into him instead of pushing through? Receive his call to rest today, and watch him fill you up in ways you don't even know you need.

Inhale Truth
Rest is not weakness.

Exhale Trust
God is my strength.

God, I'm so weary that it's hard to remember what it feels like to be truly rested. Rushing and striving have become my default setting. But I don't want to live burned out. I want to be refreshed in you. Lord, please teach me how to rest—even when life is full and messy. Show me how to release my anxious grip so I can have open hands for all you want to give me. Amen.

28

Tangled and Ready for Rescue

I will be like a shepherd looking for his scattered flock.
I will find my sheep and rescue them.
—EZEKIEL 34:12

When my soul feels anxious and tangled, I ask God for a picture—a fresh way of understanding his heart, a new way to cling to hope. Here is one of those pictures:

In my mind I saw a lamb caught in a bush. The lamb was thrashing and bleating. Thorny branches poked at her from every side, trapping her fleece and legs. The sheep had wandered away from the flock, away from the watchful eye of her shepherd. The lamb had been looking for something, chasing after something. Her wandering led to a predicament she couldn't escape.

The sheep's eyes shone with fear, exhaustion, and a touch of angry rebellion. She kept struggling, trying to free herself from the prickly confines. But she couldn't. The lamb needed saving.

Then, a voice called out to the lamb. Soon, the shepherd came running from over a hill. When he arrived, he didn't stand far off and scold the sheep or ask why she had wandered away from his protection and care. The shepherd simply climbed into the shrub. Thorn by thorn, branch by branch, the shepherd untangled the lamb. Then he picked up his lost sheep and carried her back to where she belonged.

In my heart the Lord said, This is a picture of how I feel about you. The thing that got you stuck is not too hard for me to untangle. I will always come to your rescue. There isn't a mess too big or pit too deep for my rescuing love to reach.

This is who Jesus is. He's our rescuer and redeemer. He's our savior and our shepherd. He will always come after his lost, anxious, and tangled-up lambs. He'll carry us back to the safety and security of his presence.

Stop trying to get yourself unstuck and instead call on the Good Shepherd. He's eager to come find you and carry you close to his heart.

Inhale Truth
The Lord is my shepherd.

Exhale Trust
He will rescue me.

Jesus, thank you for being our good shepherd. Thank you for coming after me when I've wandered off. Help me remember that even when I feel scared and stuck, I am not alone. You will always come. Indeed, you are always here. Wrap me in your arms today. Amen.

PEACE
PRACTICE
4

Cry

You keep track of all my sorrows.
You have collected *all my tears* in your bottle.
You have recorded each one in your book.

—PSALM 56:8

Tears are like God's built-in detox system for our hearts. When we cry, we're not just shedding stress hormones and toxins—we're physically releasing the weight of anxiety, making space for peace.[11]

Crying even helps our bodies shift from tension to rest.[12] (Isn't it amazing how God designed us for healing?) Letting our emotions flow keeps them from piling up, preventing the kind of overwhelm that leads to even more anxiety.

So don't hold back or shame yourself for feeling deeply. Let the tears fall, even if you don't fully understand why you're crying.

Jesus sees every tear, holds each one, and meets you right there in the middle of it all.

29

The Master Upcycler

We know that God causes everything to work together for the good of
those who love God and are called according to his purpose for them.
—ROMANS 8:28

My mom was a DIYer long before TV or Instagram made it popular. My favorite upcycling project she ever did happened in the wake of a massive house fire that destroyed our property. After the flames had been extinguished, our blackened backyard became a clean slate for a fresh landscape. But a lean budget meant most of my mom's suburban garden dreams had to be modified. Thankfully, her creativity and resourcefulness were not in short supply.

She wanted to ditch the concrete stoop at our back door in favor of a large wooden deck. But concrete removal is expensive. So my mom came up with a plan to repurpose the unattractive concrete into a functional retaining wall that would serve as the structural frame of the yard.

For days the neighborhood shook with the piercing grind of a jackhammer. Once the stoop was reduced to makeshift stones, my mom sorted through the debris, painstakingly matching jagged pavers to create her vision.

From a pile of rubble, a retaining wall was formed that curved around the perimeter of the yard. The lower level gave room for new grass, perfect for Easter egg hunts and summer cartwheels. The area above the retaining wall became dedicated space for plum trees, crawling strawberry plants, and purple lilies.

My mom gave purpose to destruction leftovers destined for the dumpster. In doing so, she helped usher in a new season of life and joy for our family. My mom was a salvager, a new-story writer, a creator, a broken-pieces redeemer. And that is exactly a reflection of our God. God takes what is burned and busted up and makes it beautifully purposeful.

Whether you are suffering through the blackened aftermath of your sin or from wounds inflicted by others, whether you're walking through chronic illness or anxiety, enduring seasons of depression or walking through broken relationships, you can trust that God has not forgotten you or abandoned you. In God's loving, creative hands, any fire or failure can be used to resurrect new life.

> *Inhale Truth*
> God works everything for my good.
>
> *Exhale Trust*
> I will look for his purpose and beauty.

God, so often all I can see is the rubble, the devastation, and the lack in my life. But your vision is so much greater than my limited perspective. Please take my pain and brokenness and transform it into something beautiful. Replace my anxiety with confidence in your purpose for my life. Lord, please help me partner with you in creating beauty from ashes. I want the new life you give. Amen.

30

Soul Refreshment

The instructions of the LORD are perfect,
reviving the soul.
The decrees of the LORD are trustworthy,
making wise the simple.
—PSALM 19:7

How would you describe the state of your soul today? Weary or worried? Burdened or burned out? Does your soul feel heavy or tangled or even toxic? What if your soul could be revived and refreshed so you were free from all of that? The world touts lots of solutions to our stress. Try this supplement. Do this workout. Use this face cream. Follow this guru. There's nothing wrong with taking ashwagandha or doing Pilates; God wants us to be good stewards of our bodies, and we all need complete nutrition and adequate sleep. But when it comes to the condition of our souls, there is only one unfailing source of renewal: His name is Jesus.

The great news is that soul revival isn't limited to a Sunday morning or church pew. You don't have to light a candle and read your Bible at the same time every day to encounter Jesus. God's presence is everywhere.

I feel the love of Jesus when I'm hiking shady trails in my local foothills. I see him in the dappled light streaming through a grove of twisted oak trees. I hear him in the chatter of birds and squirrels. I feel his presence in the soft breeze on my neck. I inhale him in the earthy aroma that brings grounding comfort to my often-frenzied soul.

Perhaps you have encountered God's refreshment in a timely phone call from a friend, a beautiful sunset, a moving song, or a stranger picking up your tab at a restaurant. God delights in buoying our spirits with his presence in a plethora of ways. After all, the Creator of the universe is infinitely creative! But a guaranteed way to engage with God and discover the soul revival you need is through his Word.

Scripture is God's love letter and operations manual for abundant living. The guidelines therein are not to stifle or restrict us; they are loving guardrails that will empower and protect us. All of God's holy Word— yes, even the "rules"—are imbued with the freedom, hope, and purpose we desperately need.

Trendy remedies for your soul angst and discontentment might produce "results" for a little while, but the only thing you can truly put your trust in is the living, active, and infallible Word of God. Need wisdom? Need restoration? Need a soul reset? The Lord will meet you in the pages of Scripture. Open the Word and get ready to be revived.

Inhale Truth
God alone revives my soul.

Exhale Trust
His Word is trustworthy and wise.

God, thank you for the gift of your holy Scriptures. Your words are perfect. My soul is weary, anxious, wrung out. I want to be filled up by you. Grant me supernatural understanding of your Word that I might know you more deeply and experience your love more fully today. Amen.

31

The Answer You Can Count On

Keep on asking, and you will receive what you ask for.
Keep on seeking, and you will find. Keep on knocking,
and the door will be opened to you.
—MATTHEW 7:7

I've read these words from Jesus and felt a great surge of hope. *Yes, Lord—I'm asking! I'm knocking! I'm seeking!* And yet, what about the times when the answers don't come? When the healing doesn't happen? When the anxiety doesn't lift? Was God's Word wrong?

If you've ever begged Jesus for peace in your mind or relief in your heart—but still feel stuck in the swirl of worry, you're not alone. I've been there too. Honestly, I'm *still* there some days. But here's what I've come to realize: What Jesus promises in Matthew 7 isn't a magic formula to get what we want—it's an invitation to get more of *him.*

More of his presence. More of his peace that goes beyond understanding. More of his nearness in the middle of the mess.

When Jesus told us to ask, knock, and seek, it wasn't a promise that life would be easy or anxiety-free. But he *did* promise to be with us. And that's not small comfort—it's everything.

As a mom of three teenage boys, I get how easily communication can get misunderstood. I might say one thing, but my boys hear another—and suddenly we're knee-deep in frustration. There are times when my husband and I make decisions that don't align with our kids' requests; but our wisdom is forward-thinking. We are after their long-term character, maturity, and development more than their immediate preferences.

I think that's how it is with God too. We may not always understand his timing or his ways, but we can trust his heart.

If you're feeling anxious, weary, or confused by what seems like silence, don't stop knocking; keep seeking; keep asking. Not just for answers, but for *him*.

Because more of God is always available. And more of him is always enough.

Inhale Truth
I ask, seek, and knock.

Exhale Trust
I receive more of God.

Jesus, you know the prayers I've whispered and the ones I've sobbed. Thank you that you never grow tired of my asking, are never annoyed by my knocking, and are never distant when I seek you. Remind me that your presence is not a consolation prize—it's the gift my soul needs the most. Meet me in my anxiety with your peace. Hold me steady in the waiting. And help me trust your heart even when I don't understand your ways. Amen.

32

When You Don't Want to Miss His Voice

Be still, and know that I am God!
—PSALM 46:10

Every December, the holiday hurries do their best to burn me out. Juggling Christmas parties and shopping lists, trying to remember which kid needs a five-dollar ornament and which one must bring a traditional dish for his classroom feast. It's enough to cause my anxiety to skyrocket and make me want to crawl in bed and stay there till January.

When chaos—even the kind rooted in celebration and good cheer—threatens to overwhelm me, I remind myself to listen to the voice my soul aches for. "Help me hear you, Lord," I plead. "God, what are you saying? I don't want to miss it."

Sometimes I feel anxious about hearing God's voice. Not because I doubt his ability to speak to my heart but because I question whether I'll be able to discern his voice above the noise. Life is just so loud. And it's not even about the staggering volume that comes from my three sons. I'm talking about the noise of constant information. The increase in confrontation. The perpetual bombardment of breaking news and viral videos. Divisive posts and explosive comment threads. So much fine print, so many must-see lists. My eyes blur and my ears ring—and not from twinkling lights or jingle bells. My soul and senses are overloaded.

The perpetual auditory input and content commotion have become white noise in our lives. But just because it's typical doesn't mean it's spiritually palatable. Our souls were made for stillness.

Do you feel weary from the nonstop grab for your attention? Dazed from the constant whiplash of hot trends and best deals and ten easy ways to give your kids their most memorable year ever while you avoid gaining five pounds? We need noise-canceling headphones for not only our ears but also our souls. You can quiet the noise and calm your soul by turning your attention away from the fray and to the Father. When I ask, *God, what are you saying?* his reply is often the same: *Make space for me.*

Whether you're in the thick of the holiday hustle or just burned out by the anxiety of regular life, take five minutes today to quiet your soul before the Lord. Meditate on today's verse. Receive God's invitation to be still. Surely he will meet you, steady you, direct your steps, and refresh your soul.

Inhale Truth
I choose to be still.

Exhale Trust
And hear God's voice.

God, this world can be so loud and chaotic. I'm so prone to busyness and distraction that it can be hard to hear you. Please train my ears to listen to your voice. Please guide my heart to respond to yours. Lord, show me how to make space for you—to be still with you. You know exactly what my anxious soul needs. I trust you, Jesus, to meet me where I am. Amen.

33

Let Them See You Cry

From the ends of the earth,
I cry to you for help
when my heart is overwhelmed.
—PSALM 61:2

"Mom, are you crying?" my eleven-year-old asked one summer while we were on vacation.

"Yeah, I am, buddy," I said, dabbing my face with a soggy Kleenex.

"How come? Are you sad about something?"

"I'm a little sad. But I also just have a lot of feelings, and sometimes they come out through tears."

"I understand," my tenderhearted boy said. Then he disappeared for a moment and came back with his beloved Gray Bear. And maybe I cried a little harder.

This is life with anxiety. Though I've battled this illness for years and have experienced a lot of healing, anxiety can still sneak up on me. Even on a family trip in the beautiful mountains, where the sky is deep blue and the air is fresh, my nervous system can get overloaded with noise, hormones, misunderstandings, miscommunication, and tension.

Old me would have stuffed the tears or hid them . . . even from those closest to me. But this time I told my husband I wasn't okay and needed five minutes to reset. I crawled in bed and let the tears flow. When Jude came near, I let him see my "not okay" and in doing so received the gift of a child's compassion. I wrapped my arms around my son's well-loved teddy bear and remembered that the God of all comfort and compassion wraps his arms around me. He hears my cries. He sends help.

It's reported that nearly one in three people in the United States are affected by an anxiety disorder sometime in their lives.[13] If you're suffering today, know that you're not alone. Be vulnerable with the people around you. Cry when you need to. Get support. You are worth it!

If you don't struggle with mental health, chances are you know someone who does. Validate their experience. Show compassion. Ask how you can love them well. Just be there.

Life is hard. And there is hope.

Inhale Truth
I can be honest in my overwhelm.

Exhale Trust
God hears me and will help me.

Jesus, thank you for all the ways you remind us of your constant compassion and relentless presence. From the tenderness of a child to the comfort of a teddy bear, from the glow of a fire to the wonder of a sunset, from the arms of a friend to the truth of your Word, thank you for being with me. I need you now and always. Amen.

34

Don't Get Drunk on Worry

Watch out! Don't let your hearts be dulled by carousing and
drunkenness, and by the worries of this life.
—LUKE 21:34

Isn't it striking that Jesus lists "the worries of this life" right alongside
drunkenness? Why would he do this? Probably because both behaviors
dull our minds and decrease our dependence on him. Worry, like excessive alcohol use, is often an attempt to control our feelings about things
we can't control. Both actions cloud our perspective, compromise our
judgment, and keep us from seeing God clearly.

In Luke 21, Jesus is warning people not to get consumed by the fleeting
pleasures and predicaments of this world. Time is short; the end is near.
His message is urgent: *Watch out!* He knows the trap of self-focus and
instant gratification we're prone to fall into, and he lovingly points us to
steadier footing.

What's the problem with a little worry? you might wonder. Worry makes
us hyperfocused on the temporary and distracts us from the eternal.
It's like staring at a flickering candle while missing the sunrise. Fretting over drops of rain while ignoring the ocean's expanse. When
we give in to worry, it's like fussing over pennies but overlooking the
King's treasure. Worry amplifies our fear and diminishes the way we
see Jesus.

This is why Jesus calls you to guard your heart. He knows how anxious
worry can rob you of today's joy and peace. And oh, how the Lord wants
you to experience his peace and joy in full measure!

So friend, stay alert to God's fingerprints in your life, the Spirit's stirring, and the hope of Christ's return. Let's not miss out on his message of redemption and promise of eternal life by being consumed with concerns that won't last.

When worry has become a perpetual habit, letting go can feel uncomfortable and scary. But there is nothing sweeter than learning to trust God. The way he works in our lives is so much better than the way we try to numb out or grasp for control. Surrender your worry so you can receive his hope and strength today.

Inhale Truth
Worry doesn't serve me.

Exhale Trust
I fix my mind on God.

Jesus, thank you for loving me enough to warn me of my harmful tendencies. I don't want to get lost in my worry; I want to be found by you. I don't want to be too numb or anxious to recognize your presence. Help me stay awake to what you are doing in me and around me. Teach me to release old patterns of worry for new rhythms of trust. Amen.

35

When All You Feel Is Pain and Fear

> Do not be afraid or discouraged, for the LORD will
> personally go ahead of you. He will be with you;
> he will neither fail you nor abandon you.
> —DEUTERONOMY 31:8

"We have to keep the suture site clean and protect his eyes," the urgent care doctor explained. My toddler had a sizable gash on his forehead that needed to be closed. But as soon as that crinkly medical paper went over Jude's face, his bloodcurdling cries pierced the room.

It's honestly painful to even recount—the way my tiny son screamed my name over and over. "Mommy! Mommy! Moooommmmmmy!" I assured him again and again with my voice and touch that I was near, that Daddy and I were right here. But as long as he couldn't see us, fear overwhelmed him.

Years later I still remember wanting nothing more than to rip that paper sheet off Jude's face, push the inflictor of pain away, and hold my son close. But I didn't. I didn't save my son from his terror. Why? Because that barrier was a means of protection, the person with the needle was an instrument of healing, and the distance between us was temporary. These facts were obvious to everyone in the room—except to the terrified little boy.

This is a poignant picture of how we often feel about our trials. In the moment, we can't see anything beyond our suffering. Our pain invades every fiber of our beings. Our fear crowds out our awareness of anything safe, good, or true. The feeling that we'll be alone forever is just as blinding as fluorescent hospital lights.

In our pain and fear we cry out for God, our heavenly Father. We want him to intervene, to hold us, to save us. We scream and wail, if not audibly then internally, until the reverberation of our cries racks our souls. We wonder why God doesn't come to our rescue, rip off the coverings from our eyes, and instantly heal the gaping holes in our lives.

I don't have all the answers for why we go through deep suffering. But just like I needed my son to trust that his pain would lead to healing, God invites us to trust him too.

When you cannot see the compassion in God's eyes, feel his tender touch, or hear his soothing whisper, you can trust the promise that he is still there.

He is our hope. Healing will come.

Inhale Truth
God will never abandon me.

Exhale Trust
He is right here.

God, whatever fear and feelings may overtake me, whatever scary circumstances may unfold around me, I trust that you are with me. Your presence is my security and my strength. I trust that you are always working for my good. When my anxiety blinds me or pain overwhelms me, please help me know to my very core that you are a good Father and you are near. Amen.

PEACE
PRACTICE
5

Get Outside

The heavens proclaim the glory of God.
***The skies* display his craftsmanship.**

—PSALM 19:1

Stepping outside isn't just refreshing—it's a built-in way to calm your heart and mind. Research shows that being in nature helps lower cortisol, the stress hormone, easing both anxiety and tension.[14]

The gentle sounds around you—birds singing, leaves dancing in the breeze—quiet the chaos inside, helping your body shift from fight or flight to a place of rest. Even a few minutes outside can break the cycle of anxious thoughts and give you a much-needed reset.

So step onto your porch, take a walk, or eat lunch under the open sky. Let the sun warm your skin, soak in the beauty of a sunset, or look up at the stars. And as you do, remember this:

You are never alone. God is with you, surrounding you with his peace.

36

Tell God the Truth

You will show me the way of life,
granting me the joy of your presence
and the pleasures of living with you forever.
—PSALM 16:11

Life doesn't have to be falling apart to make you feel like you are. Sometimes I'll have a week full of meaningful work, family dinners, moments of laughter, and remarkably good sleep—and still, I find myself feeling drained, anxious, or unexpectedly sad. Maybe you've felt that way too?

When my heart beats faster than it should, when worry invades the corners of my mind, when my breath is shallow, my muscles are tight, and my heart is heavy for reasons hard to name, I have learned that one of the most powerful things I can do is tell God the truth. Without hesitation, qualification, or self-judgment, I simply tell God everything I'm thinking and experiencing. Yes, he already knows. But radical honesty leads to radical freedom.

Telling God the truth is the doorway to hearing God tell *you* the truth. I like to have these conversations in writing because putting pen to paper helps me remember. Here is how one recent truth-telling conversation with God unfolded:

"Lord, I woke up feeling the weight of anxiety. My mind feels scattered and the whispers of depression tug at the edges of my heart. I don't want to be foggy—I want to be clear. I don't want to be weary—I want to be full of your energy, joy, and strength."

Then I asked him this question: "Jesus, what do you want me to know in this moment?"

Jesus said, "I am here."

It wasn't an audible voice but a clear impression in my heart. Suddenly my scattered, anxious thoughts became calm. Right then, nothing else mattered but the truth that Jesus was with me.

Then God said, "My presence brings peace—a calm anchor amid crashing waves. My presence brings security—you have nothing to fear when you're with me. My presence brings joy—deep assurance of my delight over you, no matter what else is going on. My presence brings rest—you don't have to strive, just hitch yourself to me."

Those are God's words today for you, too, friend. Breathe deep in his presence. Tell God the truth. Listen as he responds. And receive all he has for you.

Inhale Truth
God cares for my anxious soul.

Exhale Trust
Peace and joy are found with him.

God, thank you that in you I find the security, joy, and rest I need. You are my calm center, my gentle shepherd. Help me feel your presence today. I want to be radically honest with you—about my anxiety, my feelings, and my fears. Help me hear your voice in response so I can receive everything you want to say to me today and walk in your peace. Amen.

37

New Life for Dry Bones

This is what the Sovereign LORD says: Look! I am going
to put breath into you and make you live again!
—EZEKIEL 37:5

I barely made it to class on time. My second year of graduate school had just begun, and I was already wrung out from juggling a draining job and mothering three *spirited* little boys. I didn't know how I was going to make it through another semester.

To kick off English 510: Literature and the Bible, the professor read from *The Message* version of Ezekiel 37: "GOD's Spirit took me up and set me down in the middle of an open plain strewn with bones. . . . So I prophesied, just as he commanded me. The breath entered them and they came alive!"[15] In the middle of the passage, he got choked up but continued, "I'll breathe my life into you and you'll live. Then I'll lead you straight back to your land and you'll realize that I am GOD. I've said it and I'll do it."[16]

My white-haired professor cracked a smile and gently shook his head. He'd been teaching for thirty-seven years and didn't expect to get emotional, he explained. Then he said something I'll never forget:

"As we study the Bible this semester, it's not just academic—it's the Word of God. You can study the Bible, as many have, and not believe it. But I believe it. To Christians, the Holy Spirit speaks through the Word. I feel like this course would be a failure if it were only academic."

It's true; we could spend three hours every Wednesday dissecting Scripture and analyzing literature, and that would be fine. The professor would get paid, and the students would earn a grade. But my dear professor understood that the Bible isn't just another book. It's the living Word, breathed to life by the same God who made dry bones come alive and wants to resurrect something in us too.[17]

In what areas of our lives could we get by with "fine" yet miss out on the fullness of God's Word and his power to do something new? What if we believed God could breathe life into the weariness of our motherhoods or careers? What if we believed he could meet us in the middle of cancer treatment or marital conflict with living hope? What if we believed that our most barren places—like acute depression or chronic anxiety—weren't out of his reach?

Whatever your dry bones look like today, ask God to breathe new life. Then watch and see what he'll do!

> *Inhale Truth*
> God takes my dry bones.
>
> *Exhale Trust*
> He breathes new life.

God, you know how my soul is dried out. You know how my anxiety is high and my heart is parched and I've given up hope. Help me believe your Word, your power, and your goodness for my life today. Please breathe into every area of my life that is desperate for your touch. Do what only you can do. Amen.

38

The Continual Makeover

I am certain that God, who began the good work within you,
will continue his work until it is finally finished
on the day when Christ Jesus returns.
—PHILIPPIANS 1:6

Living in life's messy middle is rarely our first choice. We'd much rather move in a straight line, from a broken "before" to a spectacular "after." It's why we love home-makeover shows, right? We love to see hard work pay off—how that outdated kitchen, cracked foundation, or ugly wallpaper gets transformed into something beautiful.

But the truth is, even when the remodel is finished and the big reveal is complete, eventually that house is going to need work again. Gorgeous new countertops don't stop a plumbing issue under the sink. Stylish recessed lighting doesn't prevent the lightbulbs from needing to be replaced. And without continual upkeep, even a made-over home will one day become old and dilapidated, or at the very least collect dust and gunk from daily life and will require a good scrubbing.

What is true for a house is also true for our hearts. When we accept Christ as our Savior, Scripture says that we become new creations—it's a complete soul makeover. But having new hearts doesn't mean we never need spiritual maintenance. It's not an invitation to say, *Thanks, Jesus! I'll take it from here and see you in heaven!* Yet that's often how we proceed or what we subconsciously believe. The need for regular repairs and the occasional overhaul is part of being human.

So here's what we need to remember: God is always ready and willing to work in our lives! He's not put off by our chipped edges or the cracks in our foundations. He knows that our restoration isn't a one and done event; it's a continual process. God will not stop refining us and working out his good purpose in us. He's the master craftsman committed to our ongoing restoration and renewal until the day we see him face-to-face.

Don't resist God's hand in your life. Getting a "makeover" doesn't always feel good in the moment—it's a messy process! But what a gift that God is mindful of our rough patches and broken pieces. And he knows the exact updates and upgrades our hearts need. Indeed, he has better plans for our lives than we could dare to dream.

> *Inhale Truth*
> God is not done working.
>
> *Exhale Trust*
> He's still making me new.

God, thank you for never giving up on me. I've got things in my life that are in desperate need of repair, heart and soul projects that feel like they'll never make progress. When I feel stuck in my anxiety and run-down by daily trials, give me faith to believe that you'll always finish the good work you started in me. I trust you. Amen.

39

Put Jesus in the Picture

He existed before anything else,
and he holds all creation together.
—COLOSSIANS 1:17

The bags under my eyes matched the darkness of the sky the night I discovered I was pregnant again. Alongside the undeniable joy of new life, anxiety began to rise within me. I was already exhausted from caring for two toddlers—how would I manage another baby? I felt uncertain about the future and inadequate to handle it.

As the weeks went by and my belly grew, so did my worries. How would we fit our expanding family into our tiny rental house? How could we afford a car that accommodated three car seats? What would I do when my husband traveled and all three children needed my attention at once? The joy of motherhood felt overshadowed by my anxious thoughts. The future was daunting.

One morning, as my tiny boys played, I reached for *Jesus Calling* by Sarah Young. Desperate for hope, I turned to the day's designated reading. Written from Jesus's perspective, the first line struck me: "Anxiety is a result of envisioning the future without Me."

Noah crashed his toy cars and Elias knocked over a block tower, but amid their chaos Jesus reached into my ordinary day and reminded me that he was with me. The devotion went on to say, "Remember the promise of My continual Presence; include Me in any imagery that comes to mind."[18]

In that moment, I realized my mental images of the future didn't include Jesus at all. It was no wonder I felt overwhelmed—I was trying to navigate everything alone. But I wasn't alone. Through diaper explosions, toddler tantrums, vegetable battles, and teething troubles, as I struggled with mental health or everyday stress, whether I had extra help or was parenting solo, Jesus was right beside me.

In Colossians 1:17, Paul reassures us that Jesus "is before all things, and by him all things hold together" (CSB). Nowhere in Scripture does it say, "You, child of God, have to hold all things together."

What area of your life feels uncertain right now? Are you anxious about the challenges that lie ahead in singleness, marriage, or parenthood? Are you worried about your career, education, or retirement? If feelings of inadequacy or anxiety are weighing you down, it's time to invite Jesus into the picture. He is here to help you carry the load.

Inhale Truth
Jesus goes before me.

Exhale Trust
He holds everything together.

Jesus, thank you for holding all things together so I don't have to. I confess my worries and anxiety about the future. I feel like I have to figure it all out on my own. Help me remember that I am never alone because you are always here. May I be mindful of your presence in everything I imagine. Amen.

40

You're Never Really Alone

I will be your God throughout your lifetime—
until your hair is white with age.
I made you, and I will care for you.
I will carry you along and save you.
—ISAIAH 46:4

I leaned against the kitchen sink and sighed so loudly that the baby fern on my windowsill shuddered. It was a Tuesday morning and I was already *done* for the week. My work calendar, my daily to-do list, and my kids' sports schedules certainly weren't done, but my body and mind were *spent*. My energy and creativity—*depleted*. My belief in my ability to move through this intense season—*gone*. My resolve to keep on keeping on was crispy around every frayed edge. (And not the good kind of crispy, like perfect hash browns or onion rings. The kind that leaves a bitter, burnt taste in your mouth.)

I glanced at the sink brimming with dishes and felt the anxiety rise from my toes to my throat. I listened to the hum of the washing machine rewashing the load of towels that I forgot to move into the dryer two days ago. I hoped the mildew smell would get out. I felt the tightness in my chest . . . realized I was holding my breath . . . and exhaled long and slow.

Jesus, I need you. Every hour I need you, I prayed.

I headed back to my desk to tackle the project that was tangling my mind and knotting up my neck. Then I heard in my spirit, *I am here for you, Becky. Trust me to meet your needs. You don't have to walk this journey alone.*

Alone. How often do we slip into a mental silo? How often do we believe no one understands our struggles, no one is able (or willing) to help shoulder our burdens, no one sees how hard we're trying? Maybe no one cares? When we rehearse the refrain of "no one," we automatically exclude the most important Someone!

Instead of fixating on how alone we feel, we can shift our hearts to embrace the constant presence of God with us. Because he's already here!

When you're sleep-deprived from midnight newborn feedings or toddler nightmares, when you're overwhelmed by more work duties piled on your overflowing plate, when you're crushed by a relationship you can't fix—God is with you.

The power, the goodness, and the faithfulness of his presence never leave us.

Inhale Truth
I am never alone.

Exhale Trust
God will carry me and care for me.

*God, thank you for knitting me in my mother's womb and
being my God today and forever. It's so easy to feel alone in my
struggles and overwhelmed in my anxiety. Lift my chin, Jesus.
Whisper to my spirit. Help me see the ways you care for me
and carry me. Yes, every hour I need you. Amen.*

41

The Unwanted Cup

"Abba, Father," he cried out, "everything is possible for you.
Please take this cup of suffering away from me.
Yet I want your will to be done, not mine."
—MARK 14:36

Have you ever begged God to take something away from you? Wanted nothing more than for God to lead you on a different path? Or grant you a life completely free from the weight of anxiety?

When Jesus knew death was imminent, he pleaded with God to take away his suffering. But Jesus wasn't the first person to desperately want a change in circumstances. Think again about Joseph. Joseph cried out to God in prison. Why would the good Father allow him to be falsely accused and convicted? Why would Joseph go from the plush home of one of Pharaoh's officials to years in a cold, dark jail?

But it was from the belly of that prison that God lifted Joseph up to become the second greatest in all of Egypt, which set the stage for a dramatic family reunion with the brothers who had sold him into slavery. Joseph's life was fraught with hardship and injustice, but it was also the main stage for God's mercies and miracles. Joseph's act of forgiving his brothers for their betrayal opened the door for his father's entire family to be saved from the looming threat of famine. But I bet that's not what was on Joseph's mind for his future when he was wasting away month after month in prison.

God doesn't delight in our suffering, but he is always faithful to use it!

The night before Jesus knew he was going to be crucified, he cried out to his Father. He begged God to give him a way out of his anguish. In

Jesus's desperate plea we find a model for the most beautiful picture of surrender.

First, Jesus acknowledged who God is and what he can do: *Abba,* his intimate, available, loving Father, who can do all things and whose power is without limit. Next, Jesus made his honest request. Then, he submitted to the Father's will. Jesus recognized that his immediate desire, comfort, fear, and pain were not as lasting or significant as his Father's purpose.

Whatever circumstance feels too much to bear, whatever hardship feels too hard to endure, whatever injustice feels too great to overcome, cry out to God. Then remember who he is and what he can do! Trust that his ultimate goodness is at work in you. Today's pain just might be the setup for tomorrow's saving grace.

> ### Inhale Truth
> Everything is possible for God.
>
> ### Exhale Trust
> Not my will but his be done.

Father, please give me a heart like Jesus's. Help me see who you are, profess your power, and come to you with unfiltered honesty. Help me recognize that your ways and will are higher than mine. I surrender my life, my anxiety, and every challenge to you. Your perfect will be done in my life. Amen.

42

Beauty from Prickly Places

We can rejoice, too, when we run into problems and trials,
for we know that they help us develop endurance.
—ROMANS 5:3

I love plants—but the cactus is not my favorite. I find cacti more obtrusive than inviting, more awkward than beautiful. More than once I've had to remove painful spines from a child's hand. I adore nature and I'm plenty outdoorsy, but a cactus? Not the kind of plant I would ever choose.

One day on my morning walk I passed by a nondescript house with lackluster landscaping. But something out of the corner of my eye caught my attention. Protruding from a bulky, dull cactus was the most delicate white flower. I stopped to fully take in the impressive blossom. Creamy white petals splayed open, creating a deep center framing intricate light-yellow filaments. I had never seen anything like it. The expansive bloom wasn't just an unexpected visual delight for me; it was also a source of nourishment for a group of bees. The buzzing insects happily hovered over anthers heavy with pollen, zipping in and out of the cavernous center.

In that moment I was reminded that beauty can, in fact, be found anywhere. The ugly cactus and its one gorgeous blossom showed that goodness can sprout from something we would never choose.

I would never have chosen an anxiety disorder, but my journey through this diagnosis has allowed God's comfort and compassion to bloom in my life in the most surprising ways. Likewise, I never would have chosen to be long-term renters instead of homeowners. But despite the fact that our name is not on the house title, we've experienced the wild beauty of opening our rented doors, adding chairs to our table and pillows to the floor, and sharing with others the gift God has entrusted to our care.

Think back on your own life and the circumstances you would never choose. Can you see the beauty? Can you see the goodness that came from that job you didn't get or that challenging relationship? Can you see the blessing that sprouted from that difficult prognosis, cross-country move, or brutal season in parenting?

We serve a God who is in the lifelong business of turning ashes into beauty, weakness into strength, and death into hope! Surely he can bring goodness from unwanted places in your life.

Inhale Truth
God brings good things.

Exhale Trust
Even from prickly places.

Lord, thank you for your promise that trials produce endurance. In the midst of my anxiety, help me see the beauty and goodness you are bringing from this struggle. Just as a flower blooms from a cactus, may your comfort and compassion blossom in my life. Turn my weakness into strength and my burdens into testimonies of your faithfulness. I trust you to transform my thorns into blessings, knowing you bring hope from even the hardest places. Amen.

PEACE
PRACTICE

~ 6 ~

Hug

**A friend is always loyal,
and a brother is born to *help* in time of need.**

—PROVERBS 17:17

When anxiety starts to tighten its grip, sometimes the simplest thing—like a hug—can begin to loosen it. God wired our bodies for connection, and physical touch actually releases oxytocin, one of those "feel-good" hormones that help calm our nerves and quiet the stress swirling inside us.

Studies even show that a hug can slow your heart rate and lower blood pressure.[19] Amazing, right? Just one embrace can help your body shift from fight or flight to a sense of safety and peace.

So if you're feeling anxious or overwhelmed, don't be afraid to ask for a hug—even if it feels a little awkward or you're not sure you *want* one. That small moment of closeness can be the gentle reminder your soul needs: You're not alone. You're held. You're loved.

Let yourself receive it.

43

Anxiety Pinball

You will keep in perfect peace
all who trust in you,
all whose thoughts are fixed on you!
—ISAIAH 26:3

My thoughts can be like the shiny metal spheres in an old-school pinball machine. They ping from here to there to there, occasionally rolling slowly, only to then zip in frenetic motion from one obstacle to the next. There is nothing peaceful about pinball. The flashing lights, the incessant dings and chimes. The player must stay alert, on edge, flicking the paddles to keep the ball bouncing lest it slip into the pit.

This is what living with anxiety often feels like. I crave calm, yet I don't know how to stop playing the game of whirling thoughts. How do I stop living like it's all up to me to keep every ball spinning?

To interrupt our well-practiced patterns of frantic thinking and chaotic living, we must fix our thoughts on Jesus. To embrace the peace we crave, we must try a new way.

Peace comes from intentionally turning our thoughts to Christ. Instead of fixating on the swirling uncertainty of our fears or finances, for example—and stressing over what might happen if we stop obsessively tending to these—we can choose to turn our focus to Jesus. Instead of staying fixed in front of the pinball machine, we can step aside and invite Jesus to take the paddles of our lives.

This new posture and positioning will take practice. You'll likely find yourself back in the center, hovering over your life, desperately trying to control where the ball goes next. That's okay. Just notice your tendency, recognize your anxious grip, and ask Jesus to take your place.

And the beautiful thing? Jesus doesn't play the game like we do. He doesn't panic when the ball moves too fast or when life feels like it's slipping out of control. His hands are steady. His peace is perfect. When we release control and fix our thoughts on him, we don't just get relief—we get relationship. The kind where his nearness calms our chaos and his presence becomes the peace we've been chasing.

> *Inhale Truth*
> Jesus is my perfect peace.
>
> *Exhale Trust*
> I fix my thoughts on him.

Jesus, I long to exchange my spinning thoughts for a focused calm. I crave a kind of peace I can't create on my own. I need you. Help me break my pattern of anxious thinking and allow you to fill my thoughts and guide my heart instead. You are the Prince of Peace. Please rule over my thoughts and help me trust you. Amen.

44

Better Than Caffeine

The LORD is my strength and shield.
I trust him with all my heart.
He helps me, and my heart is filled with joy.
—PSALM 28:7

"Have you ever done an elimination fast?" my doctor asked. "Eliminating caffeine, sugar, and refined carbohydrates for a period of time can help reset your nervous and digestive systems, bringing you back to a healthier baseline." I had told her about my racing heart and intense fatigue, but a nutritional reset wasn't the treatment plan I was expecting.

Yet the truth was, I had been relying more and more on the temporary pick-me-up of coffee to try and fix my anxious, distracted, fatigued, foggy-brained state. When I couldn't think straight to complete a work assignment or help my kids with afternoon homework, I was also quick to reach for salty carbs or sugary sweets to push me through. But the assistance was short-lived. I knew I needed something different.

So I took my doctor's suggestion. As I intentionally made healthier choices—lemon tea and fresh veggies—I realized how deeply dependent I had become on comfort foods. Like a toddler constantly reaching for her soothing pacifier, I had relentless cravings for afternoon caffeine and evening ice cream. It soon became obvious to me that I needed not only a physical reset but also a spiritual one. I needed to face my habit of turning to temporary pick-me-ups more often than I turned to Jesus.

I had swallowed the socially acceptable lie that it was okay to wrap my hope around drinks and snacks within easy reach rather than reaching for my Savior. I don't think there's anything wrong with enjoying your morning coffee or a thick slice of pie. But what we're really made to crave is the satiating presence of God.

The world preaches reaching for the quick fix. Get that double-shot latte or Botox shot. Drive through for the milkshake and fries or let another Amazon delivery momentarily relieve that ache you feel inside. But nothing we can buy or eat or wear or do to fix ourselves will provide the soul comfort we really need. That job is reserved for Jesus.

I'm grateful to say my three-week reset led me to experience less anxiety, better sleep, and healthier rhythms. But even when I choose to enjoy an iced coffee or fudgy brownie, I remember that nothing can satisfy or sustain me like my relationship with Jesus.

As you navigate your own journey with anxiety, consider what temporary fixes you might be relying on. Just as an elimination fast can help reset your body, leaning into God's presence can reset your soul. When anxiety creeps in, pause and reach for the true comfort found in Jesus.

> *Inhale Truth*
> Jesus is all I need.
>
> *Exhale Trust*
> He is my joy and strength.

Lord, I confess that I've turned to food or drink or other fleeting pleasures, looking for the strength and comfort I can only find in you. Teach me to rely on you more, Jesus. I trust that your sustaining love and peace can transform my life far beyond any quick fix from this world. Help me trade my anxiety for your joy today. Amen.

45

Good News When Plans Fail

You can make many plans,
but the LORD's purpose will prevail.
—PROVERBS 19:21

I must admit, I have a love-hate relationship with this proverb. I read "You can make many plans," and I enthusiastically nod my head and offer a hearty *amen!* Plans are my favorite. I'm always thinking about what's next. My mind is constantly spinning with strategy and next steps. I plan so I can achieve my next goal. I plan so I can meet the needs of others. I plan to avoid conflict and discomfort. But planning might also be code for "I want to control what happens in my life."

Like me, you're probably happy and content when life is going the way you planned. But what happens when those plans get ruffled? Do you unravel? Does your anxiety take over? If you find yourself with tight fists, a knotted neck, and holding your breath, I get it. Bumps, detours, and dead ends can make us feel sad, angry, or consumed by worry. We want our well-made plans to unfold without a hitch. And when they don't? We can flounder.

But here's the beautiful assurance you can rest in today: Even when your plans fail, God's purpose for your life will prevail. When your strategy falls short, when you drop the ball, when someone lets you down, God's relentless goodness will not be thwarted.

I've had plans for a long-anticipated girls' retreat get derailed by a kid with the stomach flu. Yet in the midst of my disappointment, God reminded me of the gift of being a mom and that taking care of my son is an extension of God's care for us. I've had business plans not pan out, leading to feelings of failure—which God used as a catalyst to draw me into deeper dependence on him.

Seeing plans flop is never comfortable. But when your dreams or intentions don't turn out the way you hoped, God's goodness is still at work. It might feel like life is unraveling, but God never stops holding you together.

Don't allow your peace and joy to be contingent on your own plans working out; let them hinge on the steadfast love of God. So don't worry when your plans go awry, friend—God's purpose for your life is still right on track.

Inhale Truth
I hold my plans with open hands

Exhale Trust
Because God's purpose will prevail.

God, I'm so prone to worry my way to the life I think I want. But I recognize that the plans I make for myself pale in comparison to your good purpose. I don't want to put my confidence in my own scheming or striving; I want to put my trust in you alone. When my life is going smoothly and when my world is crumbling, I believe your purpose for me will prevail. I surrender all my plans, anxiety, and days to you. Amen.

46

Untangling Anxiety Through Pen and Prayer

The LORD is close to all who call on him,
yes, to all who call on him in truth.
—PSALM 145:18

My heart is often tangled—a crisscross of hopes and dreams, worries and what-ifs and never-ending to-do lists. I pray throughout the day, offering each twisted strand to God, asking him to unravel each anxious knot. I love talking to Jesus in the first moments of the morning before my feet hit the floor. I also talk to him in "Fix it, Jesus!" desperation when I'm exhausted from refereeing sibling disputes and in tired whispers as I wash the evening dishes.

Jesus is close when the phone rings with bad news, when conflict looms heavy, and when sickness persists. Wherever we are, God is never far away.

How incredible that we have full access to God Almighty—the One who created the Milky Way and microorganisms! Whether we're driving to work or running kids to school, sautéing onions or taking out trash cans, on bent knee or knee-deep in dirty laundry, in every moment of our days we have the opportunity to pray. I love knowing God hears my heart anytime and anywhere, but perhaps my favorite way to pray is through pen and page.

There is something extremely clarifying that happens when writing. Thoughts jumbled by anxiety become clearer and calmer—the instrument in my hand a conduit for naming feelings and requests I didn't even know I had. The heaviness of trials becomes a bit lighter when I remember through the rhythm of ink that the burden is not mine to carry alone. And perhaps the greatest gift in journaling is having a written record of what I prayed and how God answered!

In the haze of the mundane or seasons of crisis, it's easy to forget our conversations with Jesus. Sometimes it's not until we look back through our prayer journals that we can see the clear evidence of God's faithful hand at work. But if we don't record our requests, we might just miss the answers . . . and miss giving God the glory he deserves.

Colossians 4:2 says, "Devote yourselves to prayer with an alert mind and a thankful heart." As God's children, we can pray boldly and expectantly, knowing the Father hears us when we call. Journaling is a tool to help us stay mentally alert—eagerly awaiting his response. Then thankfulness will naturally flow out of you as you recognize all God has done and continue to trust all he will do.

Inhale Truth
God is always close.

Exhale Trust
He hears me when I call.

God, in the midst of my anxiety, thank you for being so close, always ready to hear my prayers. Help me untangle my worried heart as I call on you throughout the day. Remind me often that I am never alone. I want to experience the peace of your presence. Strengthen my faith to trust in your answers, and fill my heart with gratitude for your constant care. Amen.

47

The Teeter-Totter of Fine and Unfine

In my desperation I prayed, and the LORD listened;
he saved me from all my troubles.
—PSALM 34:6

One of the hardest things about anxiety and depression (at least for me) is not being able to always name it or explain it. Sometimes I can identify the triggers and call it out for what it is. But other times it's just tears waiting to spill out at the dinner table, heightened irritability at my children, or an unsettled spirit. It's feeling overwhelmed by simple tasks or exhausted after a full night's sleep.

I recently admitted a new wave of not-okay to my husband. "I'm struggling, but I'm fine," I said as huge tears slid down my cheeks.

"You don't look fine," he said.

And this is the tension of anxiety and depression: being simultaneously okay and undone, wanting to be seen and wanting to hide. I'm fine because Jesus has walked with me through these shadows before and he is walking with me now. I've sunk into the pit of anxiety, and I've walked the peaks of recovery. I've wallowed in the unspoken valley of depression and cried enough tears behind closed doors to lift myself up to a ledge where I could climb out. My faith is strong, yet days like this I just feel weak.

But I get up and make the coffee and cook the eggs. I play card games with my family. I plug away at the project. The grace of lived experience is knowing that I won't always feel what I feel in this moment.

I bawl my way through a novel. Fine and unfine are like two ends of a teeter-totter I can't get off. Yet I know the Scriptures. I can say all the right things. I can implement the coping strategies I learned in therapy. Sometimes it helps tremendously. And sometimes it still doesn't change the tears that flow and the mind that races and the sleep that eludes me and the sleep that beckons me.

I'll be honest: I want a quick fix, a five-step fail-proof plan. I want my knowledge and experience to seamlessly move me into permanent healing. But I'm learning that maybe healing looks like feeling the feelings and asking Jesus to sit with me in them. That's one thing we all can do today: In your okay and not-okay, just be. And invite someone to be with you.

If you're thinking about letting a friend into your darkness, do it. If you're thinking about going back to counseling or going for the first time, do it. If you just need to sit at the table and cry, do it. The struggle of anxiety and depression does not define you—but giving voice to it will let the light begin to shine in.

Inhale Truth
God is here with me.

Exhale Trust
He listens and saves me.

God, I don't want to hide or pretend I'm fine when I'm not. I want to be honest with myself, with others, and most importantly with you. Show me how you want to care for me and my anxious soul today. Hear my prayers and lead me to the healing I need. I trust you. Help me to keep trusting you. Amen.

48

Decision Paralysis

The LORD says, "I will guide you along the best pathway for your life.
I will advise you and watch over you."
—PSALM 32:8

I'm smack-dab in the middle of uncertainty. Uncertainty is not my favorite place to be. I feel like a weary traveler who has come to a three-pronged fork in the road with no map or compass to confirm which way I should go. From what I can see, each path has some bright spots as well as rocky terrain. They all are partially shrouded in shadows.

I feel stranded, abandoned, unprepared to take a step forward in any direction. Decision paralysis has its grip on me. My anxiety rises with each passing minute.

As my eyes dart from one path to the next, the questions in my mind swirl with increasing intensity. *Which way is the right way? What if I make the wrong choice? What if I can't handle what's down that path? What if my decision disappoints others?* I pile all the pros and cons and what-ifs into an anxious mountain. My clarity is obstructed by a fog that won't lift.

Have you been there? Are you stuck in the haze of uncertainty today?

Maybe you're at a crossroads in your career or a relationship. Maybe you're trying to decide whether to go back to school or spend the rest of your savings on another round of IVF or wondering how to have that uncomfortable but necessary conversation. Whatever is making your brow furrow and stomach knot up with indecision, know this: When we're faced with uncertainty, our beautifully certain choice is to turn to Jesus.

It's natural to feel the weight of a decision that will have a significant impact, and it's okay to feel uncertain and stressed. But we miss God's presence when we believe we're alone in our decision-making. Do you ever feel like it's all on you, as if everything depends on your ability to analyze incomplete information, fill in the blanks perfectly, and predict the future?

Nowhere in God's Word does it say the world rests on your shoulders. The Bible never demands that you know how to be the perfect parent, spouse, or leader. Instead, Scripture repeatedly emphasizes this truth: God is with you, he will guide you, and he generously gives wisdom when you ask.

I still haven't made my big decision. But my anxiety quiets when I remember that whatever path I take, I am not alone. Jesus is right here. He's right there with you too.

Inhale Truth
God knows my path.

Exhale Trust
He will guide me.

Jesus, you see the road I'm on and the fork up ahead. You know the weight I'm carrying and the questions swirling in my mind. Thank you that I don't have to figure it all out on my own. Quiet my anxious thoughts. Clear the fog with your peace. Guide me in your wisdom. Help me trust that even when I don't know what's next, you do—and you'll walk every step with me. Amen.

49

When You Keep Spraining That Ankle

Your right hand supports me;
your help has made me great.
You have made a wide path for my feet
to keep them from slipping.
—PSALM 18:35–36

When I was in seventh grade, I went to a super fun birthday party that turned super painful. Let's just say, trampolines are awesome . . . until they're not. My friend Miranda and I were having the time of our lives jumping together. The higher she bounced, the higher I bounced. Two times the bouncers, two times the fun—until I landed on a turned ankle. Unaware of my mishap, Miranda launched me even higher, and when I came back down on my compromised foot . . . *snap!* I crumpled into a ball holding my broken ankle.

Over the years, I've turned, twisted, strained, and sprained that same ankle more times than I can count. No matter how hard I try to protect it, it's like my ankle holds the memory of injury and keeps repeating the past.

Just like my ankle is prone to reinjury, our minds and hearts can become vulnerable to repeating patterns—like anxiety or fear—that are hard to break. Our brains develop ingrained pathways of response that are like divots in a dirt road, directing a car toward the exact same route again and again. I experience this often when it comes to anxiety. Though I've worked hard in therapy, learned coping strategies and calming techniques, and even used the support of medication, there are still times my mind defaults to anxious pathways. Anxiety begets anxiety. I trip again because I've tripped so many times before.

So how do we break free from harmful habits? Well, we can't do it alone. We need God to rescue us from our old ways. We need his help and strength to forge healthier paths.

One way to let God guide you is by pausing in moments of struggle to pray and reflect on his promises. Psalm 18 reminds us that God's hand supports us and makes our footing steady. When anxiety begins to creep in, stop and visualize God making a wide path for your feet where you will not slip. He wants to guide you and strengthen you. Let him, friend. The path ahead with him is beautiful.

Inhale Truth
God makes my path secure.

Exhale Trust
He is my help and support.

Lord, I confess that I easily fall into old patterns of anxiety, fear, and control. I don't know how to get out of these ruts. I need your help. Thank you for never leaving me. Indeed, your hand is on my back, supporting and guiding me. Please help me follow the good path you have for me. I don't want to focus on my anxiety today. I want to focus on you. Amen.

PEACE
PRACTICE

7

Rest

**You can go to bed without fear;
you will lie down and *sleep soundly*.**

—PROVERBS 3:24

Rest is crucial for managing anxiety, yet when anxiety is high, sleep can feel out of reach. Don't lose heart. Rest isn't all or nothing. Even a short nap—ten quiet minutes on your lunch break—can help your body and mind reset.

You can also take small, intentional steps to invite deeper rest. Create a calming bedtime routine—read, pray, take a warm bath, or stretch to unwind. Consider limiting alcohol and avoid caffeine after lunch, as these can disrupt your sleep. Make your bedroom a peaceful retreat—dark, cool, and quiet when possible. Stick to a consistent sleep schedule, even on weekends, to help regulate your body's rhythm. And if anxious thoughts won't let go, journal before bed to release them.

Even on the restless nights, know this: God is holding you close, watching over you, and whispering peace into your weary soul.

50

Unseen Spiderwebs

I pray that your hearts will be flooded with light so that you can
understand the confident hope he has given to those he called.
—EPHESIANS 1:18

I was hiking with my husband on one of our favorite trails. Going up, the
trail was wide and sunny, but the backside was narrow and shrouded by
trees. As we started our descent, we found ourselves caught in sticky
threads—spiderwebs.

As we traversed the tight path, we encountered more webs hanging
from trees, crisscrossing the trail. My sweet husband went ahead of me,
waving his hat to clear the path. Halfway down, I looked up and saw a
massive web hanging above us. The morning light shone through the
intricately woven silk. It was a pattern like nothing I had seen before. It
was breathtakingly beautiful, yet the thought of the creature that made
it and the victims it trapped sent a shiver down my spine.

I took just two steps forward and the web could no longer be seen. It was
wild. Only at the right angle, in the right position, at the right time could
the substantial web be detected. As I moved along the trail to catch up
with my husband, I looked over my shoulder for one more glimpse of
the great web—and it was as if nothing was there. Had it actually disappeared? Of course not. Just because it was now unseen didn't make it
any less real. At that moment the Holy Spirit pricked my heart, and I
understood that this is true not only in the physical world but in the
spiritual world too.

There are forces of both good and evil, light and darkness at work all
around us. Maybe today you're walking into the sticky threads of anxiety

or depression, distraction or discouragement. Maybe you can't detect the source but you keep running into opposition you can't shake.

As Paul reminds us in Ephesians 6:12, "Our struggle is not against flesh and blood, but against the rulers, against the authorities, against the powers of this dark world" (NIV). We're in a spiritual battle, friend. Therefore, we need spiritual discernment and strength.

Pray daily for clarity and courage. Meditate on God's Word, allowing his truth to illuminate the hidden battles you face. Surround yourself with a community of believers who can pray with you and encourage you. Remember, you are not alone in this fight. God's light is ever present. His presence is your protection. Picture Jesus on the trail with you, clearing the way. Because he's with you, you'll always be okay.

Inhale Truth
God floods my heart with light.

Exhale Trust
He is my confident hope.

God, I need your light. Please give me eyes to see and a mind to discern exactly what's going on in both the physical and spiritual world around me. I trust you to guide me and protect me. There is no struggle or anxiety I face today that is greater than your goodness and strength. Shine your light into my darkness. I put my hope in you. Amen.

51

Let Peace Be Your Teacher

*I am leaving you with a gift—peace of mind and heart. And the peace
I give is a gift the world cannot give. So don't be troubled or afraid.*
—JOHN 14:27

When you want to grow in wisdom, you spend time with people who are wise. You sit and listen attentively to their stories. You seek their counsel. You look for mentors, coaches, pastors, or teachers who have learned what you hope to learn, who live the kind of life you hope to live. Think of someone whose advice you're quick to follow because you trust that their years of experience and discernment will rub off on you.

Likewise, if you're feeling down and need a mood boost, you probably know just the friend who is sure to lift you up and make you laugh. We like spending time with people whose joy is infectious—those who see life through a lens of gratitude and hope. Think of someone whose mere presence can give you a fresh perspective.

It's smart to surround ourselves with people who have qualities we want to emulate. Presence and proximity are two of the greatest teachers. Spend enough time with someone and you will begin to look, act, speak, think, and live a little more like them.

This is exactly what we need to remember when it comes to our deep longing for peace—not just peaceful circumstances, but lasting peace for our souls. If we want to become people marked by peace . . . if we want to develop a steady spirit that doesn't unravel when plans fall apart or spiral into worry every time life gets hard . . . if we want to live rooted in peace rather than be swayed by headlines, then we must spend time with the Person of Peace.

The remedy for our anxious souls is to become well acquainted with Jesus. We've got to spend time listening to his voice, applying his words to our lives, and following his ways. But this isn't about doing more; it's about *receiving* more.

Jesus offers a gift of peace for your mind and heart—a gift available to you *right now*. Acknowledge Jesus's presence and choose to do life in close proximity with him today. Receive his peace by making Jesus the number one person you want to learn from. Jesus boldly told his followers to not be troubled or afraid—and assured them he would always be with them. When Jesus is near, there is no need to fear.

Inhale Truth
Jesus is the peace I need.

Exhale Trust
I give him my troubles and fear.

Jesus, thank you for offering what the world cannot give—peace of mind and heart. When fear rises and anxiety creeps in, remind me to draw near to you. Teach me to rest in your presence, to listen for your voice, and to follow your ways. I want to be shaped by your peace, not the pressures of the world. Help me live as your child—steady, secure, and unafraid because you are always with me. Amen.

52

God Loves What He Made

We are God's masterpiece. He has created us anew in Christ Jesus,
so we can do the good things he planned for us long ago.
—EPHESIANS 2:10

Think about the last time you were creative. Maybe you strung words together for a poem, mixed paint colors on a canvas, sculpted a piece of pottery, or baked a beautiful pie. We naturally marvel over what we make. The work that comes from our hands is precious. And that is exactly how God feels about us.

You are his masterpiece. He looks at you with awe and affection. God didn't create you by accident—he crafted you with intention and delight. He shaped you uniquely to join him in the good work he's already planned.

Sometimes anxiety can choke our belief that God can, in fact, use us for good. We think we have to fix ourselves first. But even in your sometimes anxious and frazzled, always in-process state, God sees your potential and purpose. You don't have to have it all together for him to work through you. He's ready to do good things *with you* right now.

Your anxiety, your brokenness, your [fill in the blank] do not disqualify you from being loved by God or partnering with him to bring goodness and hope to a weary world that needs him. Pause and really let that sink in. Your anxiety, or whatever challenge you face today, does not disqualify you from connecting with Jesus or being an instrument of his purpose.

You are beautifully designed and fully loved exactly as you are. Will God, as a loving Father, keep guiding and refining you? Absolutely. He's after our wholeness and healing. But be sure of this: God has been planning your days since he knit you in your mother's womb. He's appointed good works that only *you* can do, which means surely he will be faithful to equip you. Meditate on that today, friend.

> **Inhale Truth**
> I am God's masterpiece.
>
> **Exhale Trust**
> He will use me for good things.

God, you are the ultimate artist and creator. Sometimes I get so tangled up by my anxiety that I feel incapable of doing anything useful, anything with lasting impact. But I believe your Word and that you made me with intention and purpose. Indeed, I am your masterpiece. Help me to live like it! Show me how to partner with you in the good works you have planned for me. Amen.

53

Crave This

When I discovered your words, I devoured them.
They are my joy and my heart's delight,
for I bear your name.
—JEREMIAH 15:16

I have a deep love for ice cream. Soft serve in a cone or rock-hard in a bowl. I like ice cream late at night or on a hot afternoon. Chocolate peanut butter, creamy vanilla, coffee, mango, banana, rocky road— I supremely enjoy it all. My family's favorite restaurant serves the most magical coconut-pineapple ice cream alongside deep-fried banana spring rolls. The warm, crunchy cinnamon-banana goodness is meant to be the main event . . . but that silky, rich, cold, decadent ice cream is actually the star of the show for me.

You can probably describe your favorite dessert with similar enthusiasm. Or perhaps you have a more savory palate. Maybe your mouth begins to water just thinking about the perfect chicken pesto pasta with shaved Parmesan or a juicy cheeseburger piled high with onion rings and avocado. Whatever you crave, taste buds are a gift from the Lord. Amen? Sweet or salty, smooth or crunchy, it's a wonder that we can experience so many different flavors and textures. Food not only provides physical nourishment; it also offers deep *enjoyment*. Food is a centerpiece of culture, a connecting point for relationships, a focal point for holidays.

Because God made us to both need and desire food, he uses it as an effective illustration for how we were made to both need and desire *him*. In the Psalms we find encouragement to "taste and see that the LORD is good"[20] and that God's laws "are sweeter than honey."[21] Jesus declares, "I am the bread of life"[22] and reminds us that "people do not live by bread alone, but by every word that comes from the mouth of God."[23]

Most people eagerly pursue what they love to eat. You look forward to going out to dinner or making a favorite meal at home. You anticipate eating with friends, treating yourself to a special lunch, or indulging in that fun sweet at the end of a long week. But when was the last time you thought about and pursued God with the same fervor? How often do you see his Word as an amazing spread to be feasted on and slowly savored? If you're consumed by anxiety today, shift your focus to hungering for Jesus.

You were made to crave a relationship with the living God and find daily nourishment in his living Word. There's nothing else like it! Fill up with Jesus today and watch him replace your anxiety with his great joy.

Inhale Truth
God's Word is my delight.

Exhale Trust
His truth satisfies.

God, I know that I can be truly satisfied in you alone. Yet so often I run to other things. I give my time, money, and attention to things like food that have some value but offer only temporary satisfaction and pleasure. Please give me a hunger for you and your Word. Let any anxiety I feel today remind me that you are the one I really need. Amen.

54

It's Time to Share Your Struggles

In my distress I cried out to the LORD;
yes, I prayed to my God for help.
He heard me from his sanctuary;
my cry to him reached his ears.
—PSALM 18:6

When you are struggling with anxiety or depression—or really, struggling with anything—opening up to another person might be the last thing you feel like doing. Sharing is risky. You wonder whether the person you're sharing with is going to be safe, is going to understand or judge you. Will they be gentle with your tender heart?

But the bigger risk is *not* sharing.

If you never tell someone how you're *really* doing, then you're 100 percent guaranteed to never be fully known, seen, or understood. If you're not honest and vulnerable about your struggles, you can't receive the support and encouragement you need.

Opening up and confiding in a close friend doesn't have to be complicated. Simply say the words, "I'm anxious." Bravely confess, "I can't get out of bed today." Or tell someone, "I'm struggling to connect because I can't quiet my mind or calm my body enough to really engage in relationships."

By sharing what's going on, you give people the opportunity to show up for you. When they have the full context for your struggles, they can become a conduit of God's comfort. Unless you tell the truth about your anxiety, others won't be able to speak the words of understanding you need to hear or provide the support you need to keep going.

And don't forget, whether you tell someone in your life or not, you can always pour out your heart to God. Both types of sharing are a gift.

God doesn't expect you not to struggle. He doesn't judge you for feeling anxious or depressed or overwhelmed. God is compassionate and gracious. He loves you and he wants to hear from you. When we cry out to God, we find the relief that comes from simply not holding our problems in. When we are radically honest about our struggles and ask God for help, we open our hearts for his radical love to move in.

So tell God how you're really doing. He's listening.

Inhale Truth
God hears me when I cry for help.

Exhale Trust
I will share my distress with him.

Lord, I'm so used to holding it all in. I'm so used to believing that I'm better off hiding my anxiety and suffering alone. But I know that's not your best for me. I need your help. I need your help to be transparent with a trustworthy person, and I need your help to be fully honest with you. Thank you for choosing to listen to my every cry and loving me no matter what I say. Amen.

55

What Only God Can Do

Now all glory to God, who is able, through his mighty power at work within us, to accomplish infinitely more than we might ask or think.
—EPHESIANS 3:20

Sometimes I get Scripture wrong. It's a mistake we're prone to make when we unknowingly put the filter of our own understanding (or agenda) on God's Word. One verse I've done this with is Ephesians 3:20.

I've heard this verse often and am always filled with great hope. *Wow, God can do infinitely more than anything we could think to ask!* But somewhere along the way, I started focusing on the word *we*. As in what *we* could ask or think. And subtly the focus shifted to *me*. What more could *I* ask God for? What bigger thing could *I* dream up for God to do?

But that's not what this verse is really saying. It's reminding us that our perspectives are actually limited compared to God's. Even with the vast imagination and capacity for creative thinking God has given each of us, we still cannot come close to grasping all God is or all he can do in our lives. Paul, the author, is emphasizing the reality that God is at work in ways we cannot even fathom.

Several years ago I never would have dreamed of seeing my anxiety as a gift. I've mentioned this before, but it's been such a major shift that it's worth repeating. I can count anxiety a gift because it's expanded my capacity for compassion and connection with others. It's a gift because it's increased my dependency on God and taught me to come to him in my weakness and receive his strength. And that's just the beginning.

God loves working in ways our finite minds could never expect. So take a moment today to remember how God has already gone above and beyond in your life—those times when grace surprised you, when healing came slow but sure, when peace showed up in the middle of the storm. That's the kind of God we have.

Lift your chin and take a deep breath. Don't carry the weight of trying to figure it all out or dream big enough to impress God. You don't have to. His power is already at work within you. His plans are already more than enough. Your job isn't to orchestrate the outcome; it's to keep showing up, openhearted, ready to trust Jesus again and again.

Self-pressure off. God-hope on.

He's not done with your story. And I have a feeling he's going to wow you.

> ### Inhale Truth
> God's power is at work in me.
>
> ### Exhale Trust
> His best is infinitely more.

God, I want to understand your Word accurately. Please open my eyes to any ways I have misapplied it or put the focus on me. You are so much mightier, kinder, and more faithful than my human mind could ever comprehend. You can turn even my anxiety into a gift. Please wow me with your goodness and grace. Infinitely more. Amen.

56

Hope for Sorrow and Failure

My health may fail, and my spirit may grow weak,
but God remains the strength of my heart;
he is mine forever.
—PSALM 73:26

Even before the call came, I knew in my gut that something was wrong. My sister's voice confirmed that my dad had died of heart failure—alone in his apartment. The last decade and a half since that horrible day has felt like both a blink and a lifetime. As another anniversary passed, I took my tears and tissues to the garage and pulled out a box of old photos. Amid dozens of poor-quality Kodak prints, I found only one of my father genuinely smiling.

My dad spent much of his life wounded and wounding others. He had lost so much as a young man and carried that grief like spiny armor. He chased success and pleasure and ways to numb his pain. Ultimately, the pursuits of this world took a toll on his body and mind. The weight of failure and disappointment crushed his soul. But it was in this pit that he really met Jesus. My dad's flesh failed, his spirit faltered, but death is not the final word. I'll see him again.

Grief, however, doesn't disappear just because we know heaven is real. Hope doesn't cancel pain—it holds it. Even with the comfort of eternity, the ache of absence remains. And for a long time, I didn't know what to do with that tension.

I used to hide every time a fresh wave of grief swelled. Now I choose to be honest with the people who love me. I tell my husband I'm missing my dad—missing who he was and who I needed him to be. I tell my boys

I wish they would have known their Grandpa Ralph. Sharing your grief, your anxiety, your confusion, your pain—even if someone can't fully relate—opens the door for you to receive the support you need and for others to grow in compassion.

I often think about when Lazarus died—how Jesus joined the sisters Mary and Martha in their mourning. Jesus wept too. It didn't matter that Jesus knew he would soon raise Lazarus from the dead. He first entered into the grief of his friends.

Whatever you're carrying today—sorrow, regret, loneliness, or loss— God sees and knows. He doesn't ask you to hold it all together; he simply invites you to come. Let him be your safe place, your steady ground, your strength when your spirit feels weak. He will not turn away.

> *Inhale Truth*
> God sees my sorrow
>
> *Exhale Trust*
> And gives me his strength.

God, you understand the waves of grief I face. Jesus, you know what it's like to lose someone you love—the agony of waiting for healing. My longing for what I've lost (or what I never had) twists my soul into anxious knots. Thank you for seeing my sorrow and coming near. Your presence is my strength today and my hope for tomorrow. Amen.

PEACE
PRACTICE

8

Laugh

**A *cheerful heart* is good medicine,
but a broken spirit saps a person's strength.**

—PROVERBS 17:22

When anxiety feels heavy, laughter is a powerful way to lighten the load.

Laughter shifts your perspective, making overwhelming situations feel more manageable. It releases endorphins, which lifts your mood. A good laugh can also ease tension in your muscles for up to forty-five minutes.[24] (*Yes, please!*)

Humor acts like a reset button, breaking the cycle of negative thoughts and giving your mind a much-needed pause.

So, bring more laughter into your day—watch a funny movie, hang out with a friend who cracks you up, or recall a silly memory. These moments of joy are a God-gift, giving you strength to face the day. You've got this!

57

The Best Way to Start Your Day

I rise early, before the sun is up;
I cry out for help and put my hope in your words.
—PSALM 119:147

I set my alarm for earlier than my comfort prefers. I remind my kids about our no-TV-before-school rule and ask them to *please* read quietly if they wake up early. (Murphy's Law says if I get up early, someone else will too!) Before bed, I decide what scripture I'm going to read in the morning and place my journal and Bible on top of my laptop, lest I go on autopilot, forget my purpose, and fly right into work. Preparation is time protection.

As I drift off to sleep, I rehearse what is true: "The instructions of the LORD are perfect, reviving the soul. The decrees of the LORD are trust-worthy, making wise the simple" (Psalm 19:7).

Inviting God to fill our lives isn't a one-size-fits-all formula. There's no right or wrong way to spend time with Jesus. For me, I've found nothing better than starting my day in God's Word. At Jesus's feet. Pen ready. Listening, recording, remembering. He's never not shown up to meet with me.

The struggles of our lives, the crises, and the daily grind are real. The urgent things that demand immediate doing, the desirous things that draw us to their company, the attention-grabbing things that feel impor-tant in the moment but lack eternal significance all contribute to the constant push and pull of daily life. It's a noisy tug-of-war. But we don't have to live consumed by the clamor that is not God's voice.

So, before the sun has yet to run its rising course, I will come. With gunk in my eyes and a stiff morning back, I will come. When I reach for my alarm, I remind myself that I'm not getting up for Amazon or Instagram or email. As I pull the chain on my stained-glass desk lamp, flooding the darkness with light, I remind myself I'm not rising early to check more off my list. I rise for him.

Anxiety can feel like an uninvited guest that overstays its welcome. When I meet with Jesus first, my anxiety doesn't disappear—but it no longer gets the final word. When I meet with Jesus first, fear loosens its grip. The clamor of the world quiets when I let his voice be the loudest. So I rise—not for productivity, but for presence. Not to strive, but to be still.

You don't need a perfect plan or a perfect prayer—just a willing heart. Come tired. Come anxious. Come expectant. Jesus will be there.

Inhale Truth
God's Word is my refuge.

Exhale Trust
My soul needs time with him.

Jesus, I want you and I need you. Help me to choose you first and forever. Quiet the noise around me and within me so I can hear your voice the loudest. I don't rise for performance or productivity, but to be in your presence. Fill me with your truth, and steady my heart with your peace. Thank you for always meeting me here. Amen.

58

Combatting Spiritual Cynicism

Let us hold tightly without wavering to the hope we affirm,
for God can be trusted to keep his promise.
—HEBREWS 10:23

One summer during college, I excitedly shared with someone close to me about how Jesus was transforming my heart. I told her how God's Word had come alive to me, how I was beginning to grasp the depth of his love and grace, and how it was stirring me to love others more. As my passion bubbled over, she smiled and said, "Oh, I remember the fervor of college days. Enjoy the ride while it lasts."

Her words weren't harsh, but they landed hard. Was she saying my faith wasn't real? That my passion for Jesus was just a phase I'd grow out of? Doubt crept in, and my anxiety fired up. What if my faith wasn't genuine? What if after graduation I was met with the dull grind of Christian mediocrity? What if Jesus wasn't enough for my day-to-day struggles and this zeal I felt was just fleeting emotion?

Anxiety has a way of magnifying what-ifs. It turns small shadows into looming storms. Over time, those doubts created a tug-of-war in my heart—my faith pulling me toward hope and my fear pulling me toward cynicism.

But here's what I've learned in the twenty years since that conversation: Darkness will come, yet the light of God remains. The doubts that threatened to shake my faith did not diminish the truth of who God is. He is real. Jesus is alive. The Holy Spirit dwells within us and works through us—even when our hearts feel shaky.

Anxiety still shows up in my life, but I don't have to wrestle it alone. Hebrews 10:23 reminds us to "hold tightly without wavering to the hope we affirm, for God can be trusted to keep his promise." God doesn't ask us to hold on in our own strength—he holds us too. When anxiety whispers lies, we can cling to the truth of his Word.

Life will bring ups and downs, lights and shadows, vibrant mountaintops and dry deserts. We won't always feel on fire for God. But he isn't calling us to chase a feeling—he's calling us to pursue him. God is personal, present, and unchanging, even when we are overwhelmed.

If you're struggling with anxiety or doubt today, keep holding on to Jesus. Keep seeking him. And when you feel your grip faltering, trust that he is never letting go.

> *Inhale Truth*
> God is real.
>
> *Exhale Trust*
> My hope is in him.

God, thank you for the ways you have grown me, even through my struggles and doubts. Continue to grow me, Lord! Strengthen my faith so that I won't be swayed by anxiety, other people's opinions, or worldly cynicism. When fear and uncertainty creep in, help me rest in your unchanging promises. Open my eyes to see clearly your work in my life, and give me boldness to share your goodness with others. Amen.

59

Helicopter Brain

Fix your thoughts on what is true, and honorable, and right,
and pure, and lovely, and admirable. Think about
things that are excellent and worthy of praise.
—PHILIPPIANS 4:8

Before I've even opened my eyes or thrown back the bedcovers, my mind spins like a helicopter. I think about the dentist appointment that needs to be changed and the work deadline I might not meet. I think about the stupid fight I had with my husband and the uncomfortable conversation I need to have with a friend. My mind whirls in anxiety over my loved one with cancer, the wars overseas, that thing I regret, and how the landlord just raised our rent.

The centrifugal force of my thoughts circle and circle and circle, picking up speed with added feelings of uncertainty and inadequacy. Even once I recognize what's happening, it's hard to stop. I want to flip an easy switch that cuts the engine of my helicopering brain. But I can't find one. It's dizzying, discouraging, disorienting. And it's not even 7 A.M.

Can you relate?

Our thoughts are powerful. In the same way a pilot needs to be intentional, practiced, and focused on steering a massive copter, we need to take seriously the job of guiding our thoughts. That's why Paul says to *"Fix your thoughts* on what is true, and honorable, and right, and pure, and lovely, and admirable. Think about things that are excellent and worthy of praise."

Right after this encouragement he goes on to say, *"Keep putting into practice all you learned and received from me—everything you heard from me and saw me doing. Then the God of peace will be with you"* (verse 9). What we think about directly impacts our actions. And together, our thoughts and behaviors impact our capacity to receive God's peace.

Even when life is hard and the world is broken and you wake up with anxiety, even when your kid frustrates you or your roommate annoys you or your soul feels twisted up, you can always turn your thoughts to God. Think about all that is true, honorable, right, pure, lovely, admirable, excellent, and praiseworthy in him. When you do, peace will meet you.

> *Inhale Truth*
> God's peace is with me.
>
> *Exhale Trust*
> I fix my thoughts on him.

Jesus, when my mind spins with worry and my thoughts race ahead of me, help me pause and fix my gaze on you. Train my heart to dwell on what is true, honorable, right, pure, lovely, and admirable. Quiet the chaos within me and fill that space with your peace. Teach me to be intentional with my thoughts, knowing that where my mind rests, my heart will follow. I let go of my anxiety and take hold of your grace. Amen.

60

No Caveats or Conditions

God is so rich in mercy, and he loved us so much, that even
though we were dead because of our sins, he gave us
life when he raised Christ from the dead.
(It is only by God's grace that you have been saved!)
—EPHESIANS 2:4–5

If you woke up feeling condemned and frustrated at yourself for things you did (or did not do), here is truth you can stand on today: God loves you.

Don't dismiss this truth or bypass it because you've heard it forty-seven thousand times. Let it really seep into your heart, invade your mind, take root in the dark corners of your anxious soul. God loves you. He loves you when you're irritable, irritated, and irritating. God loves you when you make great choices and when you choose the lesser path. He loves you when you are full of anxiety and when you are full of faith.

God loves you. Period. No caveats or conditions. He loves you not for what you do but simply because you are his. You are his precious and chosen [fill in your name]. That fact is enough. It's enough for God, and he wants it to be enough for you.

Anytime you feel disappointed in yourself, come back to his love. Anytime you feel proud of yourself, come back to his love. Whenever anxiety feels like it's going to get the last word, come back to his love. The next time you blow it and the next time you succeed, God's love is the anchor your soul needs.

God loved us—me and you—so much that he made a way for us not to stay stuck in our sin or trapped in our anxiety. He made a way out of our distress and shame. Jesus is the way. So let all your uncertainty, hurt, discomfort, and regret be wrapped in his love.

Visualize God's love like a blanket around your frigid shoulders. The longer you stay wrapped up, the warmer you get. The comfort of the blanket makes you feel safe. Your muscles relax, your body stops shivering, and your anxiety wanes. Your soul feels at rest. In the same way a warm covering is sure to change your temperature, so too will God's love change your anxiety.

Christ's love is the covering you need. It's woven with threads of compassion and forgiveness. Stitched through with mercy, hope, and gentleness. His strength and power are embroidered by the mark of his love. Receive God's forgiveness. Forgive yourself. Forgive others. And let God simply love you today.

> *Inhale Truth*
> God loves me so much.
>
> *Exhale Trust*
> His love is enough.

God, your love is more than enough for me. Thank you for loving me, forgiving me, saving me. Help me release anything I'm holding on to that's not from you. I receive your mercy and forgiveness. I move forward, free from the grip of anxiety and guilt. Let me feel your love wrapping around me in this very moment. Your love is all I need. Amen.

61

Lemon Orzo Soup and Asking for Help

This same God who takes care of me will supply all your needs from his glorious riches, which have been given to us in Christ Jesus.
—PHILIPPIANS 4:19

God doesn't just promise to walk with us—he designed us to walk with one another too. We were made to share tears and laughter, gather around tables, and speak words that build each other up. One day when I was struggling under the weight of overwhelm and anxiety, the Spirit urged me to invite others to walk this stretch of the road with me.

I grabbed my phone and opened a group text with three friends. In little black letters, I poured out my heart, sharing all the things that were weighing me down: the technical glitches with my new business, unexpected family expenses, financial pressure, and extra work hours to try to meet the mountain of needs.

"I KNOW it's all in God's hands and every day I'm asking him to lead me by HIS strength and not my own," I texted. "But if I'm honest, I feel on the edge of burnout and overwhelm . . . and I just can't afford to be there. Will you please pray for peace and clarity and productivity (and rest) in the measure I need it?"

Just writing those words made my soul exhale.

Then the dings of replies came flooding in. Texts assuring me that I am seen. I am prayed for. I am loved. My friend Sara was also quick to offer dinner anytime I needed it. A couple of days later between shuttling one son to soccer and another to baseball, I pulled up to Sara's house. I walked through her door and immediately commented on the amazing aroma. "It's the lemon orzo soup I made for you!" she explained. In addition to nourishing homemade soup, there was sliced cantaloupe, a fresh salad, baguettes warm from the oven, cold sparkling waters, and even peanut butter ice cream sandwiches!

"This is so beautiful and generous I could cry!" I said, tears already welling as I hugged my friend.

This is the power of not alone. Soup and salad didn't instantly erase my anxiety or change my stressful circumstances, but they did buoy my heart and my hope; they pointed me back to the One whose presence changes everything. The kindness of a friend is always a reflection of the kindness of God. Open yourself up to his loving care by sharing your struggles with someone. God delights in meeting your every need.

Inhale Truth
God takes care of me.

Exhale Trust
I can ask for what I need.

Lord, teach me to be less self-sufficient and more God-dependent. I release my belief that I must do everything on my own. Thank you for designing me to need you—and others. When my anxiety is high, when my plate is too full, when I just need to know that I'm not alone . . . help me ask for help, that I might see your kindness more clearly. Amen.

62

The Gift of Repentance

Search me, O God, and know my heart;
test me and know my anxious thoughts.
Point out anything in me that offends you,
and lead me along the path of everlasting life.

—PSALM 139:23–24

As we've explored, there are many dimensions and possible causes of anxiety. Anxiety can be rooted in fear or control. Anxiety can be triggered by a cycle of worry when we focus on every worst-case scenario or what-if. Anxiety can stem from trauma, a genetic predisposition, or a chemical or hormonal imbalance.

When your mind is whizzing like a treadmill and you can't keep up or get off . . . when your heart is racing, your palms are sweating, or you have a pit in your stomach that's not from something you ate . . . when you just feel knotted up, uneasy, full of discontentment you can't shake . . . pause, breathe, and ask God: *What do you want me to know about my anxiety? Where is it stemming from? How do you want me to move through it?*

God's answer to me over the years has been different at different times. Sometimes he has directed me to evaluate my priorities and whether the way I'm spending my time reflects what I value most. He's led me in naming my fears, calling out lies I've believed, and surrendering my past and my future to him. Other times, God has prompted me to go to therapy, cry when I need an emotional release, ask friends to pray for me, and take medication when that's the support I need.

Still, sometimes an anxious soul indicates that we need to turn away from sin and turn toward Jesus. "Now repent of your sins and turn to

God, so that your sins may be wiped away. Then times of refreshment will come from the presence of the Lord, and he will again send you Jesus, your appointed Messiah" (Acts 3:19–20).

If you are willfully, or even unknowingly, engaging in thoughts or actions that do not align with God's character and his Word, your soul will know it. Sin always causes internal conflict. Internal conflict is a fast track to anxiety. But repentance is the beautiful road back to God. And when you walk in the direction and way of Jesus, you find the soul refreshment you need. So make our key scripture, Psalm 139:23–24, your prayer today, and let God lead you to greater freedom and peace in him.

Inhale Truth
God, search my anxious thoughts.

Exhale Trust
Lead me to life in you.

Jesus, thank you for forgiving me and loving me. I acknowledge my willful sins before you now. Also, please search my heart and bring to mind anything that offends you that I'm not aware of. Please wipe my slate clean. Reset my heart. Free me from my anxiety. I want to walk the path of life you have for me today. Amen.

63

The Battle for Your Heart

Guard your heart above all else,
for it determines the course of your life.
—PROVERBS 4:23

As the mom of three sons, I've watched my fair share of fantasy and adventure movies. I've seen battles between elves and orcs, superheroes and villains, knights and dragons. I've watched epic tales about wizards and warriors and powerful forces of good and evil. In each one of these movies, there is always something being guarded—something that is either powerful, precious, or dangerous.

For example, the Infinity Stones in the Marvel movies are guarded by all manner of magic, technology, bravery, and treachery. Those who guard them know the stones hold unfathomable power and indescribable danger. Or think of any story involving treasure. My family loves the movie *National Treasure* and how it depicts the incredible measures taken to hide a collection of riches too precious (and therefore too powerful) for any one man or country to possess. And in the Harry Potter stories, there are countless creatures and secrets, both powerful and dangerous, guarded by locks, spells, enchantments, hidden passages, and courageous souls. All these stories stir something in us.

Have you ever thought about what in your life is worthy of guarding? Solomon wisely wrote, "Guard your heart above all else." Why? "It determines the course of your life."

There is nothing more precious to God than your heart. Scripture tells us that from the heart the mouth speaks.[25] Our hearts are where we savor and store God's Word. Our hearts are where the Holy Spirit abides.

Our hearts are the driving forces behind what we think, say, and do—our very lives. Therefore, what we allow to influence our hearts is of utmost importance.

For years I gave others' opinions and expectations unrestricted access to my heart, which led me down a path of people-pleasing. When I've left the door of my heart wide open to fear and worry, guess what takes up residence? Fear and worry!

Our hearts have the capacity for Christlike love, culture-shifting compassion, and life-changing forgiveness. Our hearts hold the keys to our unique and powerful God-given identity, from which we can wield the power and authority of Jesus. The heart's value is without measure! But we must guard this most precious treasure with purpose and diligence, lest enemies like bitterness, envy, anger, and anxiety overtake us.

Ask God how he wants you to guard your heart today. You are so precious to him.

> *Inhale Truth*
> My heart is precious and powerful.
>
> *Exhale Trust*
> I will guard it well.

God, thank you for entrusting me with a heart that holds such immeasurable value. Help me to guard it with wisdom and courage, aware of the power it carries to shape my life. Show me what needs to be locked out and what must be let in. And may my heart always be a place where your truth and love dwell freely. Amen.

PEACE
PRACTICE
9

Engage

Taste and see that the LORD is good.
Oh, the joys of those who take refuge in him!

—PSALM 34:8

When anxiety starts to bubble up, one gentle way to calm your mind is to engage your senses. It's like an invitation to come back to the present—to notice what's real, right here, right now. Look at something that soothes you: a favorite photo, a blooming flower, the way sunlight filters through your window. Let the sound of worship music or a quiet fan hush your racing thoughts.

Feel the comfort of a cozy blanket or the steady heartbeat of your dog curled beside you. Breathe in the goodness of lavender or fresh coffee. Taste something simple and sweet—tea, a piece of chocolate, a juicy orange—and let it remind you that you're safe and held.

These small sacred moments of awareness can help settle your soul. God created your senses as gifts—receive them, use them, and let his peace meet you there.

64

When You Are Afraid

When I am afraid,
I will put my trust in you.
—PSALM 56:3

When I was newly married and my husband traveled for work, I hated being alone at night. As soon as the sun would set, fear would settle in my soul. As soon as it was dark, I'd start my routine of checking that all the doors and windows were locked. Any strange sound or vibration immediately sent my imagination into a catastrophe spiral. All night my sleep would be fitful. I was on high alert for any sign of an intruder or other danger. Peace and true rest were elusive.

During these fear loops, I would pray—but it didn't change how I felt. Over time, I discovered that my prayers needed to be as persistent as my fears. Instead of rehearsing all the bad things that could possibly happen and how I might prevent or respond to them, I needed to rehearse the truth. I needed to continually acknowledge my fears and anxieties before the Lord (there was no use denying them) and then remind myself where I could confidently direct my trust.

One day while reading my Bible, I came across a verse in Psalms that immediately tugged on my heart. These were the simple words of honesty and surrender I needed. When the grip of anxious fear was tight around my throat, Psalm 56:3 became a breath of hope. "When I am afraid, I will put my trust in you."

I have since taught this prayer to my children. It's been especially meaningful to my son who has struggled with fear of the dark, the unknown, and being alone. Together we rehearse what is true: *God is with me. I am never alone. God hears my prayers. I can trust in him.*

When fear tries to distract you, consume you, and catch you in its tenacious grip, rehearse the truth: God is worthy of your trust.

Picture Jesus right there next to you. Imagine him wrapping his arms around you. Breathe in the comfort of his presence and exhale, letting go of your anxiety and receiving his peace. Your fears may come again, but God will never leave.

> ***Inhale Truth***
> When I am afraid
>
> ***Exhale Trust***
> I will trust in God.

God, I've said it before and I'll keep saying it: You are so worthy of my trust. Thank you that my fears do not disqualify me from calling out to you. Rather, it is through my fears that I can grow in deeper trust and receive the deep peace I know you want to give me. Yes, I am anxious and afraid. Yes, I put my trust in you! Amen.

65

Before You Hide or Push Through

I look up to the mountains—
does my help come from there?
My help comes from the LORD,
who made heaven and earth!
—PSALM 121:1–2

When I'm struggling with anxiety or depression, it can be hard to know what feelings, needs, or voices to listen to. Do I first address the overwhelming laundry and piled-up dishes? Do I attend to the conflict that needs a solution or the responsibilities at work I can't put off? Or should I prioritize figuring out why I feel so sad? The push and pull of too many swirling thoughts, tasks, and competing emotions can paralyze me with indecision.

When this happens, it might seem like the best thing to do is just curl up on the couch and watch a sad movie or take a nap and never come out of my bedroom. There's a time for resting and retreating (enthusiastic supporter of naps here!). But sometimes we need to move through— not stuff down—our anxiety.

So how do you pinpoint what you really need to address most? First, ask yourself some questions:

- Can I identify what's causing me to feel anxious or depressed? (Maybe it's my circumstances, a chemical imbalance, a chaotic environment, an unresolved conflict, etc.)
- Have I taken care of my physical needs today? (Have I eaten, hydrated, slept, gotten outside, moved my body, etc.?)

- What will I wish tomorrow that I had done today? (Maybe I most need to tick off a to-do, rest, journal, pray, etc.)

Then, seek support. God is always our first (and continual) source of help. He invites us to release what we were never meant to control and trust him to fill us with clarity, courage, and strength for what he's called us to carry. But we also need to let others know we're struggling and ask for extra love, support, or accountability. For example, when I'm anxious about a huge project or deadline I believe I won't meet, I tell a friend how I'm feeling. I share a manageable goal I've set and ask for prayer. Just speaking the truth about where I'm at and where I need to go brings a bit of focus and calm to my day.

Ultimately, remember this: Help is available. You don't have to figure it out or do it all on your own. The Maker of heaven and earth sees you and will sustain you. Pause and talk to him before you try to push through. His strength is what you need.

> *Inhale Truth*
> I am not alone.
>
> *Exhale Trust*
> My help comes from God.

God, it's so easy to keep my eyes fixed on my circumstances and get tangled up in my own feelings. But I hear you calling me to lift my gaze—to live with my eyes up and heart open. Remind me that I was never meant to do this alone; I'm made to depend on you. I'm ready to receive your help today—and I'm learning that often means letting others into the hard places too. Amen.

66

Grace for Every Accusation

Let us come boldly to the throne of our gracious God.
There we will receive his mercy, and we will find
grace to help us when we need it most.
—HEBREWS 4:16

Confession: The other night I scrolled through random Facebook videos for twenty minutes before bed. Not that big of a deal. Except what felt like twenty minutes was actually three and a half hours.

When I realized what I'd done, it was too late. Too late to make a wiser choice, too late to avoid the social media time warp, too late to escape the consequence. For three and a half hours, the happy pulse of dopamine shot through my body with every sixty-second video. Dopamine is one of the "feel-good chemicals" in your brain and acts like a generous vending machine doling out snack-size doses of temporary pleasure. But the problem with snacks is that they rarely satisfy; they just make you hungry for more.

Just one more funny, heartwarming, validating, or shocking video. Just one more . . . Before I knew it, my body and mind were hooked, and I was like an addict in denial of how the feel-good craving was actually leading to a kind of self-harm.

When I finally let my screen go dark, the dopamine hits stopped. In their place, the stress hormone cortisol aggressively stepped in, buzzing uncomfortably through my veins. My eyes ached and my legs twitched and my mind raced. I couldn't get comfortable. I longed for the sleep I had chosen to avoid, and now sleep avoided me. I tossed and turned for fifteen, thirty, forty, seventy-three minutes. Restlessness and regret were my only companions. My anxiety was in full force.

In my middle-of-the-night self-made agony, my thoughts turned to prayer. Not in a super-spiritual way; my prayers were not poetic psalms or pious supplications. They sounded more like an angsty teenager or overly tired toddler.

God, I'm so mad right now. Ugh, I hate this. I hate how I feel. I hate that I did this . . . again. I feel stupid. I screwed up my sleep, and that means I screwed up tomorrow. I'm sorry. Help me.

And here's the thing about God: He always hears our cries for help. He always meets our confessions with forgiveness. And he always responds with grace. Tell God the truth today about how you're choosing your own way, and receive the mercy you need.

Inhale Truth
I come boldly to God.

Exhale Trust
I receive mercy and grace.

God, thank you for looking beyond my poor choices and seeing a heart that needs more of you. I don't want to repeat my mistakes. I need your grace for today and strength for tomorrow. Thank you, Jesus, for being accessible and merciful. May your love wipe out my shame as I keep coming back to you. Amen.

67

You Don't Have to Explain It to God

O Lord, you have examined my heart
and know everything about me.
You know when I sit down or stand up.
You know my thoughts even when I'm far away.
—PSALM 139:1–2

Do you ever feel utterly alone in your anxiety? As in, *How could someone else possibly understand what I'm going through when I don't fully understand it myself?* I've felt this way. When my anxiety is high, it's hard to identify how I feel or why I feel it, which makes it impossible to explain it to someone else. When I'm already in an anxious pit, the assumption that no one can relate to me just amplifies the feeling of isolation and despair. Have you been there?

Here's great news for today (and every day!): When no one else understands what you're going through, God does.

God knows your heart, your thoughts, every hair on your head and tear you have cried. He gets you because he made you. Jesus gets you because he left his heavenly home to take on our humanity. His flesh-and-dirt experience means he knows what it's like to live in a world full of brokenness and betrayal and disappointment, disease and death of all kinds. The fact that God knows how you feel and what you're going through doesn't instantly change, fix, or eradicate your trials. But wow, does it provide comfort.

If you feel like you need to thoroughly analyze or perfectly articulate your emotions, it's time to release that pressure to Jesus. Release the need to resolutely unravel the complexities of your circumstances or justify your situation. God already knows!

When it's hard to name or explain your anxiety, depression, or [fill in the blank], be encouraged that you don't have to convince God that your struggle is real. Let that freedom usher you into a place of deeper peace. God is the ultimate friend who knows you, gets you, and loves you. When words fall short or feel overwhelming, just rest in the security of his presence.

God already understands what you're going through. *Really.* And he loves you right where you are.

> *Inhale Truth*
> God understands me.
>
> *Exhale Trust*
> I am known and loved.

Lord, sometimes I just don't have the energy to explain what I'm thinking and feeling. In truth, sometimes I don't even understand it myself. But I don't want to be alone in the struggle. I long to be known, seen, carried. Thank you that this is exactly what you promise to do. Help me know you as you know me. Help me rest in your presence and receive your peace in exchange for my anxiety. Amen.

68

The World Would Never Tell You to Do This

Then Jesus said, "Come to me, all of you who are weary
and carry heavy burdens, and I will give you rest."
—MATTHEW 11:28

One of the most life-changing passages in the Bible, for me, is Matthew 11:28–29 when Jesus says, "Come to me, all of you who are weary and carry heavy burdens, and I will give you rest. Take my yoke upon you. Let me teach you, because I am humble and gentle at heart, and you will find rest for your souls."

It's a completely countercultural message. The world says, "Come when you're shiny and put together. Come when you have your ducks in a row and a flawless filter." The world shouts for us each to make our own way, be the master of our own destiny, be a girl boss or millionaire influencer. We're taught from a young age to make a good impression and told that practice makes perfect—which means perfection must be the goal, right?

But Jesus has a different message. He doesn't target the celebrities or the financially secure. He doesn't ask to meet with the ones with powerful corporate positions or Instagram-perfect hair. He isn't looking for the moms with the best family photos or the spouses who never argue or the teens without a rebellious bone in their bodies. Jesus doesn't give preferential treatment to the ones who are happily self-sufficient, able to meet every need and challenge they face with minimum effort and maximum success.

No, Jesus is interested in the weary ones. The ones weighed down with heavy burdens. The ones carrying the stigma of mental illness. The ones wrecked by divorce. The ones in chronic pain and perpetual sadness. The single moms and doing-their-best dads who feel constantly overworked and defeated. That's who Jesus wants. And he invites them to come. Does Jesus shame the broken and downtrodden or blame them for their struggles? No. Does Jesus promise a motivational speech or quick fix? No.

Jesus invites the exhausted and troubled ones to *come*. Come into his presence and receive *rest*. He promises to teach, to guide, to help, and to provide the rest each weary soul needs. I don't know about you, but that's the invitation I need. That's the Jesus I crave.

Friend, here's your reminder that God doesn't expect you to fix all that's broken or pull yourself together. He just wants you to come to him. In his presence you can start walking at his pace, following his ways, and finding the rest only he can give.

> ### Inhale Truth
> I come to Jesus
>
> ### Exhale Trust
> And find rest for my soul.

Jesus, thank you for inviting me to come to you just as I am—tired, anxious, and burdened. In a world that demands perfection, you offer rest for my weary soul. Help me lay down the heavy load of anxiety. Teach me to walk at your gentle pace, trusting in your humble and compassionate heart. Remind me daily that I don't have to carry these burdens alone. You are my refuge, my strength, and the true source of peace. Amen.

69

What Worry Adds Up To

Can all your worries add a single moment to your life?
—LUKE 12:25

If I had to name the worry that has plagued my thoughts, taken root in my heart, furrowed my brow, and slipped from my lips the most, it would be this: *time.* I'm constantly worried about time. More specifically, I'm worried about not having enough of it. Most days I feel like I'm fighting the clock. The ticking minutes are my nemesis, blocking me from checking off all the things on my never-ending, always-growing, forever-urgent list.

Why am I worried about time? Because I'm afraid of being behind. I'm afraid I can't do enough, which is a sign of my deeper fear: If I don't have enough time to do all the impossibly important things, then ultimately people will be disappointed in me. *I will be a disappointment.*

Worry is rooted in fear. When we don't deal with our fears in the way God intended (tell him the truth about our fears so we can then receive his truth instead), we inevitably end up in a dizzying cycle of worry. Have you ever been so worried you felt like you were going to throw up? Yeah, that kind of dizzying.

Not only can unresolved fear and worry make you feel sick, but worry creates an unintentional wedge between you and Jesus. The more you worry, the bigger the gap between God's presence and your awareness of him becomes. Therefore, we must be committed to eradicating worry from our lives. For me this looks like daily telling God, "I'm afraid I don't have enough time, so please show me the one next thing you want me to do. I accept your boundary of twenty-four hours in every day, and I trust you to prioritize my list, order my steps, arrange my schedule, and fill in all the gaps where I lack. I don't have to worry about disappointing people because I belong to you, Jesus. Help me honor you."

Worry can never add more moments to our days, but it can subtract from the joy and peace Jesus wants to give.

What is the most pervasive worry in your life? Tell God about it. Be completely honest. Ask him to show you the fears *behind* the worry. Then relentlessly exchange those fears for deeper trust in Jesus. Only when you release your worry can you fully embrace the comfort, joy, and peace of God's presence.

> *Inhale Truth*
> My worry won't change a thing.
>
> *Exhale Trust*
> But trusting God will.

God, I acknowledge that my worrying can't add a single minute to my life. I confess that I've gotten stuck in cycles of fear and anxiety; sometimes it feels like I will never be free. Show me the way to get unstuck. I want your presence to be more real than my worry. Help me trust you more and more, Lord. Amen.

70

When You're Barely Hanging On

I pray that God, the source of hope, will fill you completely with joy
and peace because you trust in him. Then you will overflow with
confident hope through the power of the Holy Spirit.
—ROMANS 15:13

I often feel like I'm living in the land of barely. Barely enough sleep. Barely enough patience. Barely keeping enough spoons and socks clean. (Seriously, what happens to all the spoons?) Barely fixing dinner. Barely getting dressed. Barely keeping my anxiety in check.

My default is to shame myself for all the barely, to "should" myself into doing better, trying harder.

Do you have a soundtrack of "shoulds"? *I should be on top of things. I should manage my time better. I should be over this. I should be okay by now. I should be more grateful, more together, more spiritual. I should be less of an emotional mess.*

But through the noise of my shame, I hear the voice of Jesus, who keeps gently reminding me that he is the God of abundance who isn't put off by my barely. When I'm barely holding on, God is abundantly able to hold me.

It's because of our barely that Jesus laid himself bare on the cross. He took all our weaknesses, sins, and failures upon his flawless self. He did it so we wouldn't have to keep living in the land of barely . . . barely enough righteousness, barely enough sacrifice, barely enough grace.

The bloody cross and the empty tomb mean any barely we face is a fleeting circumstance. Our future is secure! God's unshakable hope, his unending joy, his perfect peace—this is our inheritance! But the beautiful reality is that we don't have to wait till heaven to receive it. It can be ours today!

God's peace isn't reserved for the ones without mildew in their showers or strained relationships in their families. His joy isn't set aside for the ones who have never known the ache of anxiety or the stress of stretched finances. His hope isn't only designated for the optimists who never yell at their kids. The beauty of Jesus's love and grace is that they're poured out for all of us!

Focusing on all the barely in your life will magnify your anxiety. Focusing on Jesus will magnify the hope, peace, and joy available to you today. Turn toward him. Trust in him. And watch the hope overflow.

Inhale Truth
I trust in the God of hope.

Exhale Trust
He fills me with joy and peace.

Jesus, sometimes my lack is all I can see. Thank you for meeting me here and changing the lens I'm looking through. Thank you that I don't have to stay stuck in my not enough. Please help me release all my barely so I can receive all your abundance. Teach me to trust you more and more each day. May your hope overflow in my life today! Amen.

PEACE
PRACTICE
〜10〜

Unplug

Mark out a straight path for your feet;
stay on the safe path.
Don't get sidetracked;
keep your feet from following evil.

—PROVERBS 4:26–27

Without even realizing it, we can get swept up in the endless Instagram scroll, Netflix binge, or obligation to stay connected to work 24-7. But here's the truth: Constantly being plugged in can actually make anxiety worse. The disheartening headlines. The incessant pings. They leave our minds spinning and our souls no time to process and rest.

What if you started small? Try making dinnertime or your bedroom a screen-free zone. Power down an hour before bed and let your body unwind naturally. Turn off the nonessential notifications (you really don't need to know every time someone likes a photo). Maybe even gift yourself an hour each day—or one full day a week—without your phone.

You might be surprised by how much peace you gain when you unplug.

71

You Are Cared For and Carried

I have cared for you since you were born.
Yes, I carried you before you were born.
—ISAIAH 46:3

I was unprepared for how it would feel to see my husband holding our newborn son. His strong arms cradling our precious, pink, vulnerable babe. His adoring gaze fixed on this child who could give nothing in return but was the focus of endless love.

As our son grew, so did his father's love and care—which only multiplied with the arrival of two more sons. Over the years I've taken countless photos of Chris and our boys together: playing catch, doing yard work, and hiking our local trails. But my favorite captured moments are when a child is being carried.

Our youngest son, Jude, loved being held the most. Arms and legs wrapped tightly around his dad's waist, he would nestle his face in the crook of Papa's neck. In that position, Jude knew he was safe, loved, secure. If he was tired, Papa would carry him. If he was sad or hurt, Papa would carry him. If he was full of joy or full of fear, he knew that the best place to be was in his father's care.

This is a picture of God's love for us. But how often do we forget the Father's trustworthy arms are ready and waiting to carry us? How often do we let our anxiety, hurt, or fear cause us to isolate instead of connect? When we feel vulnerable, stressed, or scared, we think we have to just try harder rather than fall harder into God's arms.

Take a moment to reflect: What fear, hurt, or anxiety is making you lose your footing today? Instead of pushing forward on your own or resigning to defeat, let yourself be carried. Whisper a prayer, surrender the weight on your shoulders, and picture God's strong arms holding you close.

Just as Jude found safety and rest in his father's embrace, you can find the same in your heavenly Father. He has carried you since before you were born, and he will carry you still.

Trust him today—he's ready and waiting.

> ### Inhale Truth
> God cares for and carries me.
>
> ### Exhale Trust
> I can rest safely in his arms.

God, thank you for being my present, available, and trustworthy Father. Please help me bring my anxiety to you. I long to let you carry all my concerns as you carry me—show me how. Thank you for loving me in my weakness and weariness. You are my rescuer and strength. Renew my heart and mind today as I rest in your care. Amen.

72

On Earth as It Is in Heaven

May your Kingdom come soon.
May your will be done on earth,
as it is in heaven.
—MATTHEW 6:10

Often when I'm riddled with anxiety, it can be hard to pray. When my mind is racing with thoughts I can't control or when I'm feeling a swell of emotion in my chest, it can be hard to pray. When my body is depleted or my mind is exhausted or I'm simply soul weary, it can be hard to pray.

One of my favorite things to do (anytime, but especially when words are hard to find) is to pray Scripture. The Psalms are *full* of prayers—lament and thanksgiving, praise and appeal. But one of the most powerful prayers in the Bible is from the time Jesus taught his friends how to pray. This famous model is commonly known as the Lord's Prayer and is found in Matthew 6:9–13. Jesus says:

Pray like this:

Our Father in heaven,
    may your name be kept holy.
May your Kingdom come soon.
May your will be done on earth,
    as it is in heaven.
Give us today the food we need,
and forgive us our sins,
    as we have forgiven those who sin against us.
And don't let us yield to temptation,
    but rescue us from the evil one.

I love the line *on earth, as it is in heaven*. In heaven we will be fully healed, so today you can pray for healing. In heaven we will enjoy a closer-than-close relationship with God, so you can ask for his palpable presence and intimacy here. In heaven there will be no pain or tears, so you can pray for peace and comfort today.

Give us today the food we need is a beautiful reminder to ask God to provide exactly what you need. God will be faithful to give you enough for today. Enough strength. Enough wisdom. Enough patience. Enough endurance. Your anxiety can never outmatch God's provision.

Today, honor God's holy name as you pray. Ask him for what you need. Your Father is listening.

> ### Inhale Truth
> God gives what I need.
>
> ### Exhale Trust
> His will be done.

Jesus, thank you for showing me how to pray. Thank you for modeling dependency on the Father. God of heaven, you are holy. Help me honor you with my life. Please meet the needs I'm aware of and the ones I don't even know how to name. I receive your forgiveness. Help me forgive others as a demonstration of your love. I trust your goodness. I trust your will. I trust your kingdom come. Amen.

73

Honesty, Overwhelm, and Hearing God's Voice

I pour out my complaints before him
and tell him all my troubles.
When I am overwhelmed,
you alone know the way I should turn.
—PSALM 142:2–3

It's wild how easily striving can become our default. Without even meaning to, we slip into stress mode and start relying on our own efforts. We begin to believe it's all on us—to figure it out, to measure up, to keep pushing forward. Try harder. Be better. Do more. But none of that reflects the way of Jesus.

Jesus calls us to come to him when we're weary and burdened. Jesus tells us to listen to his voice—the Good Shepherd who knows exactly what we need. He reminds us that we can't earn his favor or love; we can only receive his gifts of mercy and grace.

But how do you actually move from that place of pressure and performing to a posture of surrender and trust? It starts with honesty. Just tell God where you're at. Say the quiet parts out loud. He already knows, and he deeply cares. Ask him to help you turn down the noise and tune in to his voice. Ask for grace to stop striving and start walking in step with him—one small surrendered moment at a time.

When anxiety starts to crawl up your neck, when overwhelm tugs at your heart, when sadness presses on your chest, God is near. Right where you are is right where God is. That's the beautiful mystery of his omnipresence. What a deep relief it is that you are never, ever alone. God is the faithful friend who is always ready and willing to listen to your tangled thoughts or knotted-up soul. He's the wise and loving Father who is ready to guide you and help carry your load. Simply acknowledge his presence and be present with him. Don't wish you were somewhere else—this moment is enough.

Do you long to hear God more? You can count on the fact that he longs to hear more from you too. Cultivate a practice of telling God the truth and listening to how he responds. If you need help getting the conversation started, here are five questions to ask God every day:

1. What do you want me to know or do today?
2. Is there anything in my thinking that you want to correct?
3. Where are you working in my life, and how can I partner with you?
4. What do you want me to understand about myself or about you?
5. Where are you inviting me to trust you more, and what does that look like?

Inhale Truth
I tell God my troubles.

Exhale Trust
His voice is my comfort.

Jesus, I'm so grateful I can pour out my heart to you. Thank you for listening as a trusted friend and responding as almighty God. You know the way I should go. I come to you in this moment, eager to hear your voice and follow your ways. Help me lean on your strength—not my own—and trust however you lead. Amen.

74

One Thing to Do Today (and Every Day)

O my people, trust in him at all times.
Pour out your heart to him,
for God is our refuge.
—PSALM 62:8

If I could tell you to do one thing today to find relief for your anxious soul, it would be this: Tell God the truth. Tell God the truth about how you are feeling, what you are thinking, what's weighing you down or tying your soul in knots.

If you're noticing a persistent theme throughout this book, good! The repetition is not by accident; it's a reflection of God's heart for you as expressed through his Word. When we study the Bible (or really any written work), repetition is a signal to pay attention. Telling God the truth is a repeated invitation straight from Scripture. I love how this is communicated in Psalm 62: *Pour out your heart to him.* But notice from today's verse above what precedes pouring out our hearts: trust. *Trust in him at all times.*

We are the most honest, vulnerable, and unfiltered with whomever we trust the most. God is meant to be that person in our lives. Our go-to for every rant and request, question and concern, trouble and tear. Pouring out our hearts from a posture of trust is the pathway to greater freedom through confession and therefore to deeper intimacy with Jesus.

Confession, after all, is simply saying what is true. It's not apologizing or justifying. It's not downplaying, ignoring, rationalizing, or explaining. Confession is telling the truth. We have to tell the truth to empty ourselves—expressing and releasing what we know, think, feel, perceive, and believe—so we can receive the truth back from God. This is how we experience God as the refuge of our souls. Truth telling is also an effective and necessary strategy for combating anxiety.

When we bottle up our feelings, deny how we're struggling, or ignore sin or wounds in our heart, anxiety festers. Being honest with ourselves and with God is like opening a window in a stuffy room; as fresh air makes it easier to breathe, truth telling makes it easier to receive God's peace.

Trust your heavenly Father. Tell him the truth today. Pour it all out. Rest in the unshakable love and security of the One who made you, knows you, and will never leave you or forsake you. Repeat, repeat, repeat.

> *Inhale Truth*
> God is worthy of my trust.
>
> *Exhale Trust*
> I pour out my heart to him.

Lord, teach me to live in a rhythm of confession. I want to get rid of all the anxious junk I'm holding on to and receive your love, freedom, and grace instead. Reveal to me anything that's holding me back from unhindered trust and truth telling. Be my refuge today, Jesus. Breathe fresh hope into my weary soul. Amen.

75

Stop Drinking Soul Poison

Be kind to each other, tenderhearted, forgiving one another,
just as God through Christ has forgiven you.
—EPHESIANS 4:32

When a stranger cuts you off in traffic, a friend flakes on plans, or a co-worker makes a thoughtless comment, you can usually muster up the willingness to forgive. But what about when an offense is complicated and layered and shakes you to your very core?

When wounds are profound and betrayal sears your soul, forgiveness isn't a onetime act. It's a continual *process.*

For years I have been in the process of forgiving someone whose actions deeply wounded my family. Each time I thought I was done forgiving, God would reveal another layer of hurt and resentment. I want to be free from the anxious swirl of "It's not supposed to be this way." I know cognitively that harboring hatred does not lessen another's wrongs but simply harms my own soul—yet still, it's hard to forgive.

Scripture tells us to "get rid of all bitterness, rage, anger, harsh words, and slander, as well as all types of evil behavior"[26] and follows that with the command to forgive one another. Notice the active language of "get rid of." We have to intentionally evict bitterness and anger from our hearts. It's reasonable to hate sin and injustice; God grieves when his children are mistreated. Yet unforgiveness is soul poison.

We can forgive others because God did it first. "God showed his great love for us by sending Christ to die for us while we were still sinners."[27] He doesn't hold our mess-ups against us. There is no sin too big, valley too dark, or pit too deep for the redemptive love of God. Our sins are forgiven. God's kindness is relentless. If we accept this truth for ourselves, then we must also accept it for others.

Have you ever considered that unforgiveness might be fueling your anxiety? Clinging to resentment is an illusion of control over justice and outcomes and breeds a restless, anxious spirit. Anxiety thrives on unresolved anger and grasping for control.

Forgiveness doesn't minimize the pain or pretend the past didn't happen. It doesn't let anyone off the hook—but it does set *you* free. Forgiveness is how we say, "God, I trust you with justice. I trust you with me." And in that holy surrender, anxiety loosens its grip. Peace moves in. We begin to breathe again. This is the beautiful invitation: to let go of what's been weighing you down and take hold of the freedom Christ already secured.

Inhale Truth
My sins are forgiven.

Exhale Trust
God, help me forgive others.

God, thank you for loving me despite all the ways I mess up. Thank you for forgiving me completely. Search my heart and help me acknowledge any bitterness, resentment, or unforgiveness I'm holding on to. I want your freedom. Teach me how to love and forgive like you. Amen.

76

The Gap We Try to Fill

In the night I search for you;
in the morning I earnestly seek you.
—ISAIAH 26:9

I've been feeling it again. That low-grade ache of discontentment. That inner restlessness, nagging, gnawing. Something softly knocking. That unnamed longing for something more—even on the good days when I finally catch my breath, catch up on laundry, meet the deadline, and make it to bedtime without turning into monster mommy.

I don't know why it takes me so long to recognize the remedy for my longing: God's still small voice.

Jesus is calling me to return to him, to spend time with him. Instead, I've been turning to the trap of glowing screens and the late-night doom-scroll. *Whoa, where did the last hour go?* I recede into alone time like it's the thing that can nourish my soul. Alone with my thoughts and my phone. Alone in my digital bubble. I'm searching for an insulated reprieve from all the daily demands and needs. But instead of rest, the roots of discontentment grow deeper.

Fun makeup tutorials distort my expectations for what I should look like. Political name-calling, blame, and shame twist my shreds of hope into dread. Cat photos and dance videos, social rants and perfect family photos draw me in but leave me empty. I tether myself to the noise of hundreds of "friends" I don't know beyond a screen. I long for fulfilling connection, but I just feel lonely. The blue glow is like a toxic lullaby I've trained myself to need.

The evidence of my choice to indulge in the digital downward spiral shows up the next morning in dark under-eye circles and two more snooze cycles. It's a chore to drag myself out of bed. I'm too tired and distracted to hear God call: *Come to me. Connect with me.*

Can you relate? Have you been there? Are you there today?

Take time to listen to your deepest longings. Take inventory of your priorities and how you're actually spending your time. Does your soul hunger for more? More social media, more sleep, more viral videos, more home organization, more activities, or more mindless TV isn't going to cut it. We were made for a different kind of more.

We were cut out for divine connection. Created for intimacy. Hand-picked for relationship. Sculpted for surrender. Wired for worship. We've each got a God-sized gap that nothing else can fill. It's time to resist what pulls us away from the Gap Filler and instead press into him.

> *Inhale Truth*
> Only God can satisfy.
>
> *Exhale Trust*
> I will seek the One I need.

Jesus, I'm sorry for the ways I've tried to soothe my soul with things that can't satisfy. Quiet the noise inside and around me, so I can hear your voice again. Help me crave your presence more than mindless scrolling and temporary escapes. Draw me back to you—my peace, my rest, my more. Amen.

77

Jesus Isn't Afraid of Your Dirt

Since I, your Lord and Teacher, have washed your feet,
you ought to wash each other's feet.
—JOHN 13:14

When I was a little girl, I suffered from terrible warts on my feet. My best friend did gymnastics, which I thought was the absolute coolest. When she invited me to go to a class with her, my first question was "Can I wear socks?" The answer was no, so I declined. I couldn't stand the thought of other kids potentially seeing something I was so insecure about.

In high school, I ran cross-country. One time I ran so hard that I fainted right as I crossed the finish line. As if that wasn't bad enough, as soon as I came to, I puked. I was mortified that my boyfriend saw the whole thing. I wanted to crawl in a hole.

When we feel flawed, weak, or embarrassed, we don't want to be seen. I've felt the temptation to hide when I'm fragile after surgery, when my anxiety is spilling over, when I've said hurtful words, and when my face is blotchy from tears. I'd rather cover up my mess and stress than be seen in the middle of it. Do you know what I mean?

In our pain and unpleasantness, our tendency is to hide. It's uncomfortable—vulnerable—to let someone bear witness to our weakest moments. We live in a world of masks and filters, where we subtly believe only the cleaned-up versions of ourselves are worthy to be received. But this is not what Jesus teaches. Jesus is not afraid of our dirt. He loved people so much he was willing to bend low to wash the filth from their feet and reach in to clean the muck from their souls. Jesus loved the woman at the well, Zacchaeus in the tree, and the paralyzed man by the pool.[28]

But the proof of Jesus's love doesn't start with *forgiving* the woman's sexual sin, *redeeming* the traitorous tax collector, or *healing* the man's crippled legs. It actually begins with *seeing*. The love of Jesus sees people. His love acknowledges our struggles, our pain, and our plights.

Jesus was not afraid to touch the one with leprosy, look into the eyes of the one caught in adultery, or spit in the dirt and scoop up mud to smear on the eyes of the one without sight. He wasn't afraid of Mary's tears or her hair wiping his feet. He was not afraid to weep.

This is who Jesus was when he walked the earth, and this is who he is today. You don't have to hide in your hurt or your shame. Jesus is here to bend low and love you right where you are. Receive his love so you can then love others.

> ### Inhale Truth
> Jesus reaches for me in my dirt.
>
> ### Exhale Trust
> He makes me clean.

Jesus, you know the ways I'm prone to hide, especially when my anxiety is high. Help me not to hide from you. Thank you for accepting me with my proverbial dirty feet and loving me enough to not look away. You see me and reach for me, just as I am. I need you. And I want to be like you. Lead the way. Amen.

PEACE
PRACTICE

〜11〜

Serve

**The generous will prosper;
those who *refresh others* will themselves be refreshed.**

—PROVERBS 11:25

One of the most beautiful ways to calm our anxious hearts is by looking up and looking out—serving someone else right where we are. When we take the focus off our own worries and pour love into another's needs, it reminds us that we're not alone in our struggles.

Helping someone else pulls us out of the cycle of worry and into the joy of giving. It brings purpose, connection, and fulfillment—things anxiety can't touch.

You don't need grand gestures—simple acts of kindness are just as powerful. Make a meal, be a listening ear, lend a hand. An encouraging note or texted prayer can make a huge difference in someone's day.

As you show up for others, you might just find your own peace growing too.

78

When the Day Already Feels Like Too Much

If your instructions hadn't sustained me with joy,
I would have died in my misery.
I will never forget your commandments,
for by them you give me life.
—PSALM 119:92–93

Have you ever felt defeated as soon as your eyes fluttered open? Like you already wanted to give up before your feet hit the floor or you poured your first cup of coffee? Whether it's clinical anxiety, situational stress, or fresh grief, feeling beat down and overwhelmed can ruin a day before it even begins.

This is when it can feel hardest to turn to God's Word—and is exactly when we need to the most. As we read earlier, Jesus, recalling words from Moses, said, "People do not live by bread alone, but by every word that comes from the mouth of God" (Matthew 4:4). The nourishment we desperately need is found in God's sustaining truth.

But Jesus also said, "I am the bread of life" (John 6:35). So, do we need bread or don't we? Both metaphors point to the truth that Christ alone can sustain us. God's aim isn't that we just get by in life but that we truly thrive. So when we are withering with stress and anxiety, Scripture offers a spiritual feast! Christ's table is laid with *all* joy, wisdom, and strength. What would it look like for you to be filled up with the hope and peace of Jesus? Imagine being fully satisfied with his peace and nourished by his strength.

No morning will be too overwhelming or night too despairing as long as you cling to God's Bread of Life, his living Word.

The trends of the times, the whims of friends, the expectations of co-workers—all these things will change. But God never changes. His Word stands firm through the ages. His goodness never wavers. God isn't going anywhere, which means we can confidently say,

I will not be overcome, but I will be overjoyed.
I will not be burned out, but I will burn with Christ's love.
I will not be discounted, but I will be counted faithful.
I will not be rejected, but I will rejoice in who I am in Jesus.

If you're on the brink of a breakdown or feeling immobilized by misery, remember the source of life. Reach out to God—surely he is already reaching out to you.

> **Inhale Truth**
> God's joy sustains me.
>
> **Exhale Trust**
> His Word gives me life.

God, teach me to love your Word and recognize my constant need for it. Thank you that you don't want me to stay stuck in my misery, my anxiety, or my overwhelm. Help me recognize my hunger for you. Teach me what it means to delight in your instruction, abide in your presence, and receive the Bread of Life. I know you will provide everything I need. Amen.

79

Flip the Script

Give all your worries and cares to God, for he cares about you.
Stay alert! Watch out for your great enemy, the devil. He prowls
around like a roaring lion, looking for someone to devour.
—1 PETER 5:7–8

One surefire way to an anxious soul is to fixate on your mistakes. Want to really wreck your peace and wreak havoc on your heart? Go ahead and visualize every terrible, horrible, no-good, very bad thing you've done or what-if that might happen. Let those guilt- and panic-induced scenarios play out in your mind on repeat. You surely won't be able to fall asleep at night or focus during the day. And exhaustion is an essential ingredient for the perfect recipe of stress and anxiety.

Of course, I'm being facetious. We never pursue stress and anxiety as if they're a prize to be won. Yet sometimes we need to flip the script to understand where our subconscious patterns and willful actions lead. Recognition is the first step to course correction.

Begin to recognize when you slip into cycles of ruminating on past missteps you can't change or future situations you can't control. Then consider what you would say to a friend who was in your same situation. Would you judge her as harshly as you judge yourself? Would you think her shame was well placed?

Chances are, you would extend kindness and compassion to someone you love. So practice speaking to yourself the way you would speak to a friend. It's really hard to receive God's grace when we refuse to give grace to ourselves.

And remember this: The enemy is like a prowling lion, looking to devour your joy, peace, and trust in Jesus. Stay alert! Remember that our struggles are not against flesh and blood but against rulers, powers, and authorities of this dark world.[29] But in Christ we are more than conquerors![30] Fretting does not lead to freedom. Jesus wants you to be free of guilt and shame that are not yours to carry.

God cares for you. Let his peace wrap around you. Lean in. Rest in him.

Inhale Truth
Worry doesn't serve me well.

Exhale Trust
I give all my cares to God.

God, help me recognize the destructive thought patterns in my life, as well as the enemy's destructive schemes. Teach me to battle well for inner peace, which I know is found only in you. Thank you for caring for my heart, mind, body, and soul. Thank you for being available to hold all my cares today in your compassionate and powerful hands. I don't have to spin my mental wheels about tomorrow because my spirit is at rest in you today. Amen.

80

You Don't Have to Save Yourself

I wait quietly before God,
for my victory comes from him.
—PSALM 62:1

Imagine David writing these words or perhaps speaking them aloud to steady his own heart: "I wait quietly before God." It's as if he's coaching himself, reminding his soul to trust in God, to anchor in the truth. This is a powerful example for us. Because when we don't *feel* the truth, we have to *declare* the truth. Speak it out. Preach it to ourselves until our hearts catch up with what we know.

Declaring the truth is especially vital when you struggle with anxiety. You might *believe* God is in control, but your anxiety tells you a different story. Your anxiety tells your mind and body that you are frantic, worried, or in danger.

I love the Christian Standard Bible version of this verse, which translates "wait quietly" as being "at rest." It's in our restless, anxious moments that we must train our minds to focus on the truth. To proclaim, "I am at rest in God alone."

David also reminds us that our victory—our salvation—comes from God. This is such good news! You are not saved by mastering your anxiety. You are not saved by what you accomplish in a day or what other people think about you. You are not saved by being spiritual enough or meeting someone else's expectations. Your eternal victory rests in Jesus Christ. Every struggle you face today ultimately has a good ending because we know how God's story ends!

Take a deep breath and remember that no anxiety or worry, no struggle or striving can keep you from the rest God offers. Jesus chose you. He died for you because he loves you. And he conquered death to bring life to you. Declare the truth. Preach God's goodness to your own heart. Rest in that. Rest in him today.

Inhale Truth
I cannot save myself.

Exhale Trust
My rest and rescue come from God.

Jesus, thank you for loving me, saving me, and giving me the soul rest I need. When I feel anxiety crawling up my back or pounding in my chest, when worry and what-ifs swirl in my mind, please help me remember that I can rest in you. Show me what it looks like to wait quietly before you today. My well-being and my salvation are secure in you. Hallelujah! Amen.

81

Asking *What* Instead of *Why*

When they call on me, I will answer;
I will be with them in trouble.
—PSALM 91:15

I'm pretty sure my middle son's first word was "Why?" Since he was a toddler, Elias has had an insatiable need to understand. *Why are rocks hard? Why do we have to eat vegetables? Why do people cry? Why won't you answer all my whys?*

I love his curiosity, but there are times I've had to say, "I'm not going to explain the full why right now. You just need to trust that what I'm telling you is enough for today."

That's not what inquisitive kids—or anxious hearts—want to hear.

Oh, how like Elias we can be. We cry out to God, begging to know, *Why is this happening? Why do I have to wait? Why don't I see you working?* Sometimes we ask from a place of hopeful expectancy, but often our whys come from fear—our deep need for control in a world that feels anything but predictable or safe.

Lately, I've had my own list of whys. *Why does someone I love have cancer? Why does suffering persist in my family? Why does it feel like every step forward is met with another setback?* Maybe you have a why list too.

But here's what I'm learning: Shifting from asking *why* to asking *what* makes all the difference. Instead of *God, why is this happening?* I ask, *God, what do you want me to know about this?* God may not always explain his reasons, but he will always reveal his love.

When I ask, *God, what do you want me to know about this uncertainty?* he answers, *I go before you and will be with you; I will never leave you nor forsake you.*[31]

When I ask, *God, what do you want me to know about this heavy burden?* he answers, *I am close to the brokenhearted and save those who are crushed in spirit.*[32]

Asking God *why* can leave us spinning in frustration. But asking *what* will always lead us closer to his heart. I want my son to trust that I see a bigger picture than he does. God wants the same for us. So today, take a deep breath. Release the whys that keep you tangled in worry. Ask God *what* he wants you to know. Then listen. Receive. Respond.

Surely, he is working for your good.

> ### Inhale Truth
> God will answer when I call.
>
> ### Exhale Trust
> I trust what he tells me.

Father, you see my anxious heart and hear all my questions, yet you gently invite me to trust your presence more than my need to understand. Thank you for being with me in the hard places and working for my good, even when everything feels uncertain. Today I let go of control and rest in the truth that you are faithful, near, and always listening. Amen.

82

Pulled Apart

Don't worry about anything; instead, pray about everything.
Tell God what you need, and thank him for all he has done.
—PHILIPPIANS 4:6

I long for less anxiety and more peace. Less trying to hold my life together and more leaning deeply on Jesus. Less striving and more surrender. Are you nodding your head with me?

Every time I think about the tension between the anxiety I experience and the peace God promises, the Lord always brings me back to one thing: *prayer*.

The apostle Paul told us to stop worrying and pray about everything. Many Bible translations use the word *anxious* in place of *worry:* "Do not be anxious about anything" (NIV). It's important to note that this is referring *not* to a mental health disorder but to the kind of anxiety that is general to all people.

Interestingly, the Greek word here for "anxious" is *merimnaó,* which means to be divided or pulled apart.[33] Isn't that an apt description for anxiety? When our circumstances pull us in different directions, when we feel pulled by the wounds of our past or the uncertainty of the future, when our thoughts are divided between God-dependence and self-reliance, anxiety rises.

So what is the antidote for being anxious? *Pray about everything.* How? *Tell God what you need, and thank him for all he has done.*

God always wants us to be honest. As a parent, I wholeheartedly understand this desire. When my children hide their feelings, their fears, or their failures from me, they aren't able to feel fully seen, understood, or supported. Vulnerability is the bridge to trust. Tell God what's tangling your soul. Tell him how you need his healing and wisdom, his clarity and courage. Then, thank him.

Gratitude primes our hearts to remember who God is and all he's already done. It shifts our focus from worry to the One worthy of our trust. We don't have to be thankful *for* every specific circumstance, but we can be thankful *through* it.

What happens when we pray with honesty and praise? "Then you will experience God's peace, which exceeds anything we can understand. His peace will guard your hearts and minds as you live in Christ Jesus."[34]

God's peace in place of our anxiety? Yes, please.

> *Inhale Truth*
> God's peace guards my heart.
>
> *Exhale Trust*
> I will pray and give thanks.

Jesus, you know the ways my heart feels pulled in a hundred directions. Help me pause the spiral and turn to you. I choose gratitude and trust. Thank you for the circumstances in my life that are a catalyst for deeper surrender. I give you my anxiety in exchange for your peace. Thank you for always being near. Oh, how I need you. Amen.

83

From Wallowing to Receiving

Why am I discouraged?
Why is my heart so sad?
I will put my hope in God!
I will praise him again—
my Savior and my God!
—PSALM 42:11

As I write this, I'm supposed to be camping in Big Bear, but instead I'm home sick with Covid-19. My family is waking up to fresh mountain air and will spend the day playing under towering pines, riding bikes with the lake breeze at their backs, and huddling around the campfire with friends. I'm waking up with a sore throat, stuffy nose, and pounding headache and will spend the day in bed with my trusty thermometer and a box of Kleenex.

This camping trip is a family tradition—my favorite week of the year. We've been trekking up the mountain since our boys could barely roast their own marshmallows and had to be carried on hikes. Now they are teenagers and taller than I am. I'm keenly aware of how precious and fleeting time together is. And how I'm missing it.

Yet Jesus gently nudges me to bring my disappointment and frustration to him. There is no feeling he hasn't felt. He knows what it's like to surrender his hopes, expectations, and discomfort to the Father. So I tell Jesus that I'm sad and discouraged. I tell him I'm bummed about not getting our annual family photo on the big log and not being able to watch my boys skip rocks on the lake. I let myself grieve the memory making that didn't happen, and I admit the anxiety I feel because of it.

And then I remember to ask God one of my favorite questions: *What do you want me to receive?*

Maybe that's the question you need to ask today too. In the middle of your sadness, disappointment, or what-if anxiety, shift your focus from what you don't have to what God wants to give you.

After walking through this process with Jesus, I can't help but see all that God's given: the comfort of being sick in my own bed, joy over my husband and sons still sharing this special time together, and the kindness of a neighbor who dropped off groceries. This was just the beginning of the provision God wanted me to receive.

I was tempted to wallow in my sickness and disappointment. But wallowing is like an anxiety fuel station. A quick pit stop might be unavoidable, but staying too long will delay you from receiving God's best. Bring your honest feelings to Jesus so you can move past wallowing and be free to receive his fresh hope for today. Praise him!

> ### Inhale Truth
> I release my disappointment.
>
> ### Exhale Trust
> I put my hope in God.

Jesus, thank you for meeting me in my sadness and discouragement. Dwelling on my disappointment fuels my anxiety; help me dwell on your goodness instead. I'm so grateful I can be honest with you. I choose to release my disappointment and take hold of every good thing you have for me. I trust your will and your ways. Amen.

84

Do You See Jesus?

> In one of the villages, Jesus met a man with an advanced case of
> leprosy. When the man saw Jesus, he bowed with his face to the
> ground, begging to be healed. "Lord," he said, "if you are willing,
> you can heal me and make me clean."
>
> —LUKE 5:12

Before we get to the miracle, there are four words we must examine: *The
man saw Jesus.* Though keenly aware of his great need, the man with
leprosy lifted his eyes from his circumstances and set his gaze on the
One in front of him. He recognized Jesus's presence *and* his power.
When we're in need of healing, the first step is to *see* Jesus.

Next, the man responded to what he saw with respect and awe—*he
bowed with his face to the ground,* a posture of humility and adoration.
Only then did he humbly yet boldly ask Jesus for what he needed—*to be
healed and made clean.*

But look at the risky words he said first: *Lord, if you are willing.* Imagine
his desperation and physical suffering: burning skin, disfigured hands
and feet, swollen nerves. In the first century A.D. there were no pharma-
ceuticals to treat bacteria, reduce inflammation, or lessen chronic pain.
Jesus was his only hope.

Surely the man was also suffering from the social ramifications of his
disease. Leprosy ostracized people from community, excluded them
from worship, and disqualified them from relationship. Those with leprosy were pushed to the outskirts, ignored, denied. In other words, the
disease had stolen everything. No one could save him—but Jesus. The
afflicted man acknowledged Jesus's power to heal yet submitted himself

to Jesus's will. It wasn't a matter of Jesus being *able* but whether he was *willing*.

I love the Lord's response: "Jesus reached out and touched him. 'I am willing,' he said. 'Be healed!' And instantly the leprosy disappeared" (Luke 5:13). *He reached out.* Jesus responded to the man's presence and his plea. *He touched him.* How personal, intimate. And take note of this: Jesus touched the man *before* he was clean. Others deemed him untouchable, infected, written off, too far gone. And in *that* reality, Jesus reached out!

That is still who Jesus is and what he does. He is not afraid of your anxious soul, your mess, your sickness, your brokenness, or your sin. There is nothing you have or haven't done that can make Jesus keep his distance.

He is the God who comes near, reaches out, wipes clean our past, cleanses our souls, and heals our bodies—immediately on earth or eventually in heaven. Either way, our first step is to see him.

> ### Inhale Truth
> Jesus, I see you.
>
> ### Exhale Trust
> If you are willing, heal me.

Jesus, help me lift my eyes from my pain and truly see you. Give me a heart that bows low in awe, even as I come boldly with my need. I trust your power, but more than that, I trust your heart. Thank you for being the God who reaches out— before I'm clean, before I'm whole. Lord, if you are willing, heal me. Amen.

PEACE
PRACTICE
12

Give Thanks

Enter his gates with thanksgiving;
go into his courts with praise.
Give thanks to him and *praise* his name.

—PSALM 100:4

Gratitude is a highly effective way to quiet anxiety. When we shift our focus from the weight of our worries to the gifts God has already given us, it's like taking a deep breath of God's peace.

Start small—thank God each morning for three things, whether it's the warmth of your coffee, a moment of quiet, or the reminder that he's with you. Write them down or speak them out loud. And then, before you close your eyes at night, name three more.

The more you make gratitude a habit, the more you'll feel anxiety loosen its grip and joy begin to grow.

God's goodness is all around you—keep your eyes open to it shining through even hard and unexpected places.

85

Tap, Tap, Tap

Pray in the Spirit at all times and on every occasion. Stay alert and
be persistent in your prayers for all believers everywhere.
—EPHESIANS 6:18

I started playing the trumpet in first grade—a dream come true to follow
in my very cool older sister's musical footsteps. But it took persistence.
My initial request was ignored. I was too young, and my family couldn't
afford lessons. But after months of begging, my mom finally relented on
one condition: I had to actually be able to play. My mom and the music
teacher thought I wouldn't have the lung capacity required for a trumpet, since most children don't start playing until fourth grade. So surely
I'd have to give up and wait.

But I wasn't like other kids. One day after my sister's private lesson, I
picked up the brass horn and blew with all my seven-year-old might! It
wasn't a particularly pleasant tune, but it was loud. My mom lost her bet,
and I began my musical training.

Making sound came easily to me, but finding my rhythm took work.
Whenever I sat down to practice, I turned on the metronome and tapped
my foot to the ticktock, ticktock. Though I could read music and play
notes, I still had to learn to follow the beat. So there I sat, not playing—
just tap, tap, tap. My sisters teased me for this, but I kept at it, trying to
connect my eyes to my fingers to my brain. Tap, tap, tap.

With practice and persistence, I stopped needing the metronome. My
pre-playing tapping became less frequent, and I was able to jump right
into the music. Eventually, I didn't have to think so much about what I
was doing; I could simply enjoy the gift of playing.

Our prayer journeys can be a lot like my trumpet journey. We might hold our Bibles and have things on our hearts to say but still hesitate. We have the green light to talk to God, yet sometimes the rhythm of prayer feels hard to find. Maybe you find yourself tapping your foot in shame, feeling unworthy to bring your needs to God. Maybe you keep tapping because you're distracted or anxious or worried you'll say the wrong thing.

Prayer is a pathway directly to God's heart. God's heart is a pathway directly to his peace. And God's peace will transform your anxious soul.

So practice praying! Pray when it feels awkward. Pray when it feels hard. Pray when you're tired, frustrated, and wondering whether it will ever make a difference. Just keep praying. Your persistence will pay off. The great Teacher is right there beside you and within you. Follow his lead, and one day you'll discover what a natural joy it is to pray.

Inhale Truth
Tap, tap, tap.

Exhale Trust
Teach me, Lord, to pray.

God, thank you for inviting me to pray at all times—no matter what I'm feeling or what circumstance I'm facing. I don't want to pray by my own rhythm or agenda; I want to pray in your Spirit according to your will and your ways. Make me teachable and persistent. Don't let my anxiety get in the way. Rather, help me enter your presence so I can access your peace. May joyful prayer become my new favorite practice. Amen.

86

Moved with Compassion

When the Lord saw her, his heart overflowed with compassion.
"Don't cry!" he said.
—LUKE 7:13

Jesus was on his way to a new village with his disciples. As they approached the village gate, they encountered a funeral procession. Imagine the scene: The atmosphere was charged with emotion. The culture of communal grief was on full display. Men carried a coffin—a box too small for a grown adult. Women clustered together—shuffling, wailing, arms flailing. Untold pain collectively groaned, and a whole village showed up to bear witness for the son whose life ended too soon.

In the midst of all this commotion, the Lord saw *her*. Jesus looked through the crowds, looked past his own plans for the day, and saw one woman, one widow, one grieving mother. And his heart overflowed with compassion. How beautiful is that?

Compassion is the core of who God is. It's one of the first things God declared about himself. When he spoke his name to Moses on Mount Sinai, he said, "Yahweh! The LORD! The God of compassion and mercy!" (Exodus 34:6). Compassion is always on God's heart when he sees his children.

Out of an overflow of compassion, Jesus drew near to the one who was hurting most. He spoke to the woman. He entered into her grief. He touched the coffin where her dead son lay. This is who God is. He is not distant or disengaged. He is the God who sees. Compassion moves him. He is the God who speaks and comes near. Jesus is the one whose words, touch, and presence change *everything*.

That day Jesus brought the dead boy back to life. Today, he wants to resurrect something in your life. Maybe your hope is dead or your joy is dull. Maybe you're swallowed by fear or shackled by anxiety. Maybe you feel like a nameless face in the crowd and doubt that Jesus would ever see your anguish or hear your lament.

Let me tell you, dear one. He sees *you*. His compassion overflows for *you*. God is ready to have a life-changing encounter with you. Look up. Listen for his voice. Let him meet you right where you are with all that he is.

Inhale Truth
God is full of compassion.

Exhale Trust
He sees me.

Jesus, thank you for being the God who sees me. Thank you that my tears are never invisible to you. My loud cries and soft groans do not fall on deaf ears. When my heart is heavy or hope feels lost, remind me that your compassion is not far off—it's overflowing for me right now. You don't rush past my pain; you draw near, you speak, you restore. Help me to lift my eyes and believe that you can still resurrect what feels dead inside me. Amen.

87

True Life After Dashed Dreams

Then he said to the crowd, "If any of you wants to be my follower,
you must give up your own way, take up your cross daily, and follow
me. If you try to hang on to your life, you will lose it. But if
you give up your life for my sake, you will save it."
—LUKE 9:23–24

As a teenager I dreamed of going to Stanford. My best friend's dad was an alum, and her brother was a current student. On a campus visit, I easily pictured my future self walking the lush grounds, studying in the impressive libraries, and donning the collegiate sweatshirt that would show I had made it.

When I applied during my senior year of high school, I was confident. I was valedictorian of my class, and I had a long list of involvement in activities, athletics, leadership, and community service. I had top grades and impressive accolades. I thought my future was perfectly mapped out.

And then . . . I didn't get in. I was devastated. This wasn't the way my story was supposed to go. But that deep disappointment eventually turned into a tremendous blessing because it shifted my focus. I slowly realized that the life I *truly* wanted wasn't about being accepted into an elite university—it was about embracing God's love and his plan for me.

Life rarely unfolds the way we envision it, and those detours can amplify anxiety and be hard to accept. But even when our well-made plans or big dreams get dismantled, hope is not lost. Jesus invites us to follow *him*. We don't get to follow Jesus based on our perfect résumés, qualifications, or clean bills of health but based on our willingness to surrender our own ways.

Following Jesus means letting go of control and trusting that God knows what's best for our lives. It's about picking up the cross God calls us to carry—not chasing after the world's fleeting promises of comfort, success, or security. True peace and purpose are found when we're walking in Christ's shadow, reaching for his hem, keeping in step with him.

Friend, you don't have to figure out your entire future. The life Jesus offers is far better than anything we can plan for ourselves. It's not wrong to have dreams or be successful, but these things don't define us—Jesus does. Life to the fullest is found in following him, wherever he leads.

Inhale Truth
Life in Christ is better

Exhale Trust
Than getting my own way.

Jesus, I want to follow you. I come with open hands, surrendering my plans and dreams. Help me trust your path, even when it looks different from what I imagined. When anxiety tries to take over, remind me that true peace is found in following you. Teach me to let go of control and embrace the life you have for me. Thank you for your love that never fails and your guidance that never wavers. I choose to follow you, knowing that your way leads to true purpose and joy. Amen.

88

Don't Write Off Rest

Let's go off by ourselves to a quiet place and rest awhile.
—MARK 6:31

In the midst of a busy season of preaching, healing, and deliverance, Jesus invited his disciples to pull away. He called them to pause their good work and receive the gift of rest with him.

Mark 6:31 in the CSB says, "Come away by yourselves to a remote place and rest for a while." My first thought is: *Yes, please, and hallelujah! That's exactly the invitation I need!*

Jesus, I'll gladly leave behind the demands of daily life. Time alone? Even better—I'm all for quiet over crowds. A remote place? If that's code for a tropical island or cozy mountain cabin, count me in. And rest? My spinning mind, heavy heart, and weary soul are desperate for it. Best of all, it's not rushed. I don't have to hurry back to doing.

My whole being exhales at the idea of such a lavish invitation.

Yet I wonder how the disciples responded. They had just returned from their ministry tour. Surely some were anxious to get back on the road for the sake of the kingdom. Some probably missed their families and wanted a day off to kiss their wives, hug their mothers, or catch up with the friends they left with their fishing nets. Maybe some, in their weariness, simply thought going away felt like too much work—wouldn't it just be easier to stay put?

Sometimes even good invitations can end up feeling like obligations. But Jesus isn't focused on our convenience or packed calendars; he cares most about giving our souls what they truly need—rest with him.

Spiritually, rest moves us from a place of self-reliance to God-dependence. When we cease doing, we can more easily hear God's voice and respond to his leading. Letting Jesus direct my time always lightens my heart and increases my peace. Physiologically, chronic anxiety is linked to elevated levels of the stress hormone cortisol. Rest, especially quality sleep, helps regulate cortisol levels, reducing the body's stress response.[35] Rest also helps your brain process memories and emotions, making it easier to handle anxious thoughts.[36]

What if you accepted God's invitation to spend time resting with him? That could look like taking a weekend retreat or retreating to your laundry room for five minutes of quiet. God doesn't care about the logistics—he cares about simply being with you.

Get away with Jesus today. Time with him is soul restoring and always, always worth it.

Inhale Truth
I will quiet my soul

Exhale Trust
And rest in Jesus.

Jesus, thank you for calling me to get away with you. This can feel like an impossible invitation to accept but one I desperately need. I recognize that I don't have to impress you with more doing—I can press into you with more being. Teach me to care for my body, mind, and soul the way you do. You wired me for rest. I trust your ways. Amen.

89

King Jesus and Toilet Conversions

Now he is far above any ruler or authority or power or leader or
anything else—not only in this world but also in the world to come.
—EPHESIANS 1:21

I accepted Jesus into my heart when I was five years old . . . while sitting
on the toilet. True story. I remember the day clearly. I was in our upstairs
bathroom, legs dangling as I sat looking at the 1980s flower pattern on
the linoleum floor and thinking about the truths I had heard in Sunday
school. And it all clicked.

I asked Jesus to forgive all the wrong stuff I had done and come into my
heart so I could live with him forever. As a spunky, independent kid, I
hopped off my porcelain throne, flushed my sins away, and put Christ
rightly on his throne. (Yes, I've always loved metaphors, and this still
makes me smile.) I washed my hands and went downstairs to tell my
mom the good news.

Nearly forty years later, I still marvel at the creativity of God, who pur-
sues us and calls us to himself in countless ways and places. (I also think
God definitely has a sense of humor.)

But what's not so humorous is how often I've taken Jesus off his throne in
favor of lesser kings. Pride, productivity, approval, fear, anxiety, control—
each of these has spent time as ruler of my life. And the results have been
disastrous.

When we give Jesus authority over our lives, he leads with compassion,
directs with truth, protects with peace, and loves unconditionally. But
when we give power to anything (or anyone) else, anxiety is bound to

follow. Our hearts were not made to trust in earthly rulers, celebrities, or government leaders. We were made to trust the One who formed our bodies in our mothers' wombs, calls us by name, and cares for our souls.

Today is a good day to ask yourself, *Who is on the throne of my life?* Let the Holy Spirit reveal to you the ways you're being led by someone or something other than him. Perhaps pleasure or worry is on the throne. Maybe you've been exalting a political party or others' opinions. Maybe you've started to prioritize comfort, chase success, or even focus too much on your own limitations. It's never too late to put yourself under the authority of Jesus.

Today is a good day to adopt a childlike faith that is curious, teachable, and ready to grow. What greater peace could we receive than knowing Jesus is on the throne?

Inhale Truth
Jesus is my king.

Exhale Trust
All authority is his.

Jesus, I confess that I've put other things on the throne of my life instead of you. Please forgive me. There is not a person, possession, or position that is worthy of my worship and devotion besides you. Help me embrace the truth of your love with a childlike faith—pure, humble, eager to know you and be loved by you. Don't let anxiety or fear hinder me from surrendering to you. Please rule in my heart and direct my steps today. Amen.

90

Trusting God with Soup

*Don't be selfish; don't try to impress others. Be humble, thinking of
others as better than yourselves. Don't look out only for your own
interests, but take an interest in others, too.*
—PHILIPPIANS 2:3–4

As I served chicken tortilla soup to my family, I thought about my
neighbor—the one who lives alone, doesn't often cook, and might not
have eaten much that day. I considered sharing our dinner with her but
hesitated, wondering, *Will there be enough?* I had planned for this simple meal to feed my family for two nights, and giving some away might
mess with my schedule.

Let's be honest—don't we often think this way? If I give my time here, I
might not have enough for myself later. If I'm generous with my money
now, there might not be enough for future needs. If I share my [choose
a resource], I might not be prepared for what tomorrow brings.

This is a scarcity mindset. And the world preaches it loud. We're constantly hearing messages of "there's not enough" and "look out for yourself." We live in a self-centered, protect-your-own-interests culture, and
this message reaches deep. The result? We become afraid of not having
enough. This fear creates anxiety whenever we have to choose between
helping others and taking care of ourselves. Most of the time we choose
to self-protect.

But self-protection isn't the way of Jesus. He laid down his life for us,
and he calls us to do the same for others. This doesn't mean that we
become doormats or throw healthy boundaries out the window but that
we ask ourselves some hard questions: *Do I trust that Jesus will take care*

of my needs? Do I live as if he's the true owner of my time, my money, my soup?

In his letter to the Philippians, Paul encourages believers to care for others, look out for their interests, and adopt the same attitude as Jesus. The Word tells us that when we exchange our worries for gratitude, God's peace will cover us, beyond anything that makes sense![37]

After a few moments of wrestling—and remembering God's goodness to me—I dished up a bowl of soup for my neighbor and filled baggies with fresh grated cheese and tortilla chips. When she opened the door, her face lit up. After a delightful conversation and a warm hug, she thanked me again. Back in my kitchen, I put our leftovers into a container. The remaining soup fit perfectly—any more and it would have overflowed.

In that moment God whispered to my heart, *When you trust me, I make everything enough.*

Inhale Truth
God cares for me.

Exhale Trust
So I can care for others.

God, thank you for everything you've given me. You are my provider and my protector. I want to steward well all that you've entrusted to my care. Teach me to live softhearted and openhanded. Dismantle any selfishness, fear, or anxiety that could keep me from trusting you. I want to experience more of your love and peace so I can share it with others. Amen.

91

Hope in the Wilderness

I feel sorry for these people. They have been here with me
for three days, and they have nothing left to eat.

—MARK 8:2

I've heard the story of Jesus feeding the five thousand since my childhood days of Sunday school flannelgraphs. So as an adult when I got to Mark chapter 8 and read the story of Jesus feeding the *four* thousand, I did a double take. Was this a misprint?

The stories bear a striking resemblance: A crowd gathers to hear Jesus's teaching; he sees the spiritual *and* physical needs in front of him; tangible resources fall short; Jesus gives thanks for what they have; and a miracle of multiplication comes from mere loaves and fish.

But here's what is so beautiful to me: Jesus was no less able and willing to satisfy the needs of *this* crowd just because he had done the same for others.

In Genesis 16, we find the story of Hagar, a woman who had been mistreated and abused, trying to escape her circumstances. It's in that place of desperation that God meets her. She is the first person in the Bible to give God a name. She calls him El Roi, "the God who sees me" (verse 13).

Whether it was a solitary woman on the run or a crowd of thousands, God drew near to those who were desperate for him and showed compassion. His compassion is not limited or exhaustible. The blessing given to one or a multitude doesn't exclude *you* from also receiving God's kindness and care. God is attentive to the needs of his people throughout *all* generations.

In the wilderness, God heard Hagar's cries of distress and gave her the gift of hope through a promise. Roughly two thousand years later, in another wilderness, Jesus saw the hunger of four thousand people and gave them the gift of hope through provision. Now, more than two thousand years after that, the same God—Father, Savior, and Spirit—hears *your* cries and sees *your* needs. He is ready and willing to meet you in *your* wilderness with the gift of hope through his presence.

So when anxiety over your bleak-looking circumstances rises, look up. Christ is coming for you. His compassion never fails.

> *Inhale Truth*
> God sees my needs.
>
> *Exhale Trust*
> His compassion will meet me.

El Roi, thank you for seeing me right where I am. Thank you for caring about not only the state of my soul but also the physical needs of my body. You know my wilderness and where I need the hope of your promise, your provision, and your presence. Don't let anything stand between us. I'm ready to receive a miracle! Amen.

PEACE
PRACTICE

13

Refuel

**The LORD will guide you continually,
giving you water when you are dry
and *restoring your strength.***

—ISAIAH 58:11

Friend, what you put in your body really does affect how you feel, especially when anxiety tries to take the reins. When you nourish yourself with good, wholesome food, you're not just filling your belly—you're fueling peace, clarity, and strength for whatever your day holds.

Choosing real, nutrient-rich foods like fruits, veggies, whole grains, and healthy fats is more than a health move—it's an act of kindness toward your mind and body. These small choices can help steady your emotions, support your brain, and even calm inflammation.

But don't get overwhelmed. Just start where you are. Drink another glass of water. Swap that sugary snack for almonds or an apple. It's not about perfection—it's about progress.

Each nourishing choice you make is one step closer to a more grounded, grace-filled you. You're doing better than you think. One small step at a time.

92

Gratitude in the Grind

I will praise you, LORD, with all my heart;
I will tell of all the marvelous things you have done.
—PSALM 9:1

Over the past nine months, my anxiety has been less intense than at any time in the last nine years. It's been ages since I woke up with the crippling tightness in my chest that once greeted me every morning. I can't even remember the last time I cried from a deep, unexplainable sadness. God has done amazing things for me!

When I reflect on my journey with anxiety, I'm overwhelmed with gratitude for how God has sustained me through the darkest valleys and led me to places of healing, hope, and true rest.

Yet if you asked me on any given day whether I feel stressed or on the brink of overwhelm, my answer would probably be a resounding *yes*. Healing doesn't always mean the absence of pain. Hope doesn't always mean life is easy. But here's what we need to remember: Facing challenges or feeling stretched doesn't mean we aren't making progress.

It's easy to get caught up in the daily grind and forget to give thanks. We often miss God's presence in our lives and the ways his strength shows up in our weaknesses. We need to lift our eyes from our current struggles to see how far we've come.

I don't know how anxiety might show up in my life tomorrow, next month, or next year. But here's what I do know: When I take time to look for God's faithfulness, make praise a priority, and share the wonderful things he has done, my joy increases and my peace deepens. It's like making spiritual deposits in the bank of my soul. The interest and dividends accrued are priceless!

Take time today to reflect. How has God sustained you through a struggle? What evidence of growth in your life do you see? (Even small progress is still progress!) Pause and consider how God has shown his power in the mighty mountaintops and mundane messes. And give thanks. There is always a reason to praise the Lord!

> *Inhale Truth*
> God has done great things for me.
>
> *Exhale Trust*
> He is worthy of my praise.

Lord, you are so faithful—even when I cannot see it. Give me eyes to see. Even if today feels weighty with suffering or anxiety is clouding my vision, I trust that you are still here and still working in my life. Help me recognize your fingerprints of healing and grace. Give me the opportunity to boldly tell others about the marvelous things you have done for me. I love you. I need you. I trust you. Amen.

93

Keep Confessing Your Fears

I hold you by your right hand—
I, the LORD your God.
And I say to you,
"Don't be afraid. I am here to help you."
—ISAIAH 41:13

How do we break free from the cycle of fear? How do we stop fixating on our weaknesses and limitations? Through confession. Confession makes space for God's truth to replace our worries, doubts, and misconceptions. Fears out, truth in—shifting our focus from self to Savior.

I keep talking about fear because it keeps creeping in. Battling fear through confession is something we must keep practicing. When I confess to God that I'm afraid I don't have what it takes—to finish a task, to stop being defensive and love my husband, to set aside my irritability and be patient with my kids—I'm actually opening a door. This door leads to the peace and joy of God.

When we bottle up our fears in the interior chambers of our hearts and minds, guess what happens? The fears fester and grow, crowding out God's goodness and truth. Confessing fear defuses its power and allows God to come in and do his beautiful and freeing work.

Confession doesn't have to be complicated. Simply pray, "God, I'm afraid of . . ." or "God, fear is making me believe that . . ." Tell God how you see him, yourself, and others. Tell him how you see your circumstances, and then ask him to tell you what *he* sees.

I spent one early morning having this kind of conversation with Jesus. I told him everything I was afraid of that day. These are the words he impressed on my heart:

I know you feel weary and overwhelmed. Those feelings aren't obstacles for me. If I've given you work to do, people to love, and ways to serve, then I'll surely provide what you need to partner with me. Let your anxiety go. Let me carry it for you. I see all you do, all you care about, all you hold. Now see me—see how I'm carrying you. I'm holding you. I'm working in, through, and for you. I'm right here with you. Live like it.

Dear one, these words are for you too.

Being honest with God about your fears opens your heart to receive compassion that calms your soul, truth that steadies your mind, and love that comforts your heart. Let go of your anxiety and cling tightly to his words. With Jesus we have nothing to fear.

> **Inhale Truth**
> I give God my fears.
>
> **Exhale Trust**
> I receive his love and help.

God, thank you that on the other side of my fears is deeper intimacy with you. I want to be honest with you so I can fully receive from you. Help me embrace the practice of confession—not because you're mad at me but because you want to free me from my fears. Help me recognize what's holding me back from trusting you. Speak to my heart today, Jesus. Amen.

94

Margot Makes Me Smile

Yesterday, I bought an eight-dollar plant from Trader Joe's. Her beauti-fully curved, dark green leaves sit in a white textured pot on my kitchen windowsill. Every time I wash my hands or do the dishes, my little plant brings joy to my day. I loved her so much that I happily announced her name was Margot. My sons, however, thought Margot was a lame name. One suggested Kevin would be better.

Today, I chose to make myself a protein-packed pasta salad for lunch. Instead of grabbing a quick snack, I boiled water and cooked red lentil noodles. I added chopped yellow bell pepper, celery, shredded carrots, crumbled feta, diced lemon chicken, turkey summer sausage, Italian dressing, and a little salt and cracked pepper. One son said it looked gross. Another said they would eat it if it didn't have celery.

My sons are wonderful, and we often joke around. But there was a time when comments like this would have made me second-guess myself. *Was buying a new plant a waste of money? Should I have made a lunch they liked instead?*

It's easy to shape our lives around everyone else's needs. For sixteen years, I've made meals to match my family's tastes and pushed aside my own. I've made sure others have shoes and clothes that fit, while I keep wearing underwear with holes. (Anyone else?) In loving my people well, I've sometimes forgotten to care for me too.

But you're never pushed aside or forgotten by God.

If you're always putting others first, maybe it's time to remember that caring for yourself matters too. Self-care is not selfish—it's a way to receive God's love. You are his beloved, and he delights in giving good gifts.

Simple choices—like adding a plant to your space or making a nourishing meal—can be powerful tools for easing anxiety and honoring God. Foods that support your body and mind really do make a difference. (Quick and easy isn't always kind to ourselves.)

So, go ahead—buy the flowers. Enjoy nourishing food you love. Receive God's goodness in the small things. God smiles when we do. (And I'm pretty sure he's a fan of Margot and celery.)

Inhale Truth
I am God's child.

Exhale Trust
I'm worthy of good gifts.

God, I want to love and serve others well—but I also want to think rightly about what it means to care for myself. Show me how to see self-care the way you do. Help me to lean into small, meaningful things that nurture my heart, ease my anxiety, and add joy to my day. Thank you for the simple ways I get to receive your love right where I am. Amen.

95

Faith That Sings in the Dark

Around midnight Paul and Silas were praying and singing
hymns to God, and the other prisoners were listening.
—ACTS 16:25

Ah, a little midnight prayer and song—how lovely. Continue reading and
we see that other prisoners were listening, and it hits—Paul and Silas
were in prison!

It had not been a good day. Paul and Silas were stripped, beaten with
rods, flogged, and thrown into the inner dungeon. To make extra sure
they didn't escape, their feet were clamped in stocks.[38] What crime had
they committed to deserve such brutal treatment? None. They had cast
a spirit out of a slave girl, which angered her masters because this spirit
made them money.[39] Their greed turned into rage, which sparked a riot,
and alas, Paul and Silas landed in jail.

And after all *that,* they chose to praise God.

Imagine being in Paul's and Silas's shoes. You're faithfully serving God—
sharing the gospel, helping the hurting, setting people free. And what
happens? You're falsely accused, beaten, and thrown into prison. It
would've made total sense if they cried out in confusion, asking God
why. If they felt frustrated, even angry, that he didn't shield them from
the pain. Honestly, we wouldn't blame them for wondering, *Is this really
what obedience gets us?*

But instead of raging at God or wallowing in resentment, Paul and Silas
turned their hearts to prayer and worship. And that choice changed everything. For probably the very first time, praises echoed in those prison

walls. Their worship didn't just shift their own perspective—it transformed the entire atmosphere. It brought peace and strength to their souls and led the jailer and his whole family to salvation.[40]

You might never be falsely imprisoned like Paul and Silas, but chances are, you've felt beaten down by life, wounded by the world, and worn thin by disappointment. Maybe you've poured yourself out in obedience, only to watch things unfold in ways that are nothing like you'd hoped. In those moments, the real question becomes this: *Will you stay stuck in the pain and anxiety, or will you lift your eyes and choose praise?*

Praising God might feel like the last thing you want to do when you're at your lowest. But here's the thing—God's goodness doesn't disappear in our pain. And sometimes, choosing praise right in the middle of the mess becomes the very thing that shifts something deep in our souls . . . and maybe even stirs hope in someone else who's watching too.

> ### Inhale Truth
> Even in my trials
>
> ### Exhale Trust
> I will sing God's praise.

God, give me faith like Paul and Silas! I want to live not by the feelings of my flesh but by the convictions of my heart. No matter what happens in my life, no matter how anxious I feel, Lord, you are worthy of my worship. Give me a new song even on the darkest nights, that others might hear the hope I have in you. Amen.

96

Don't Skip the Banana

> The Holy Spirit produces this kind of fruit in our lives: love,
> joy, peace, patience, kindness, goodness, faithfulness,
> gentleness, and self-control.
> —GALATIANS 5:22–23

I love fresh fruit. If I had to pick just one food group to eat for the rest of my life, it'd probably be fruit. But I have mixed feelings about fruit salads. I'm all in for tangy mango, juicy watermelon, sweet grapes, and snappy blueberries. I'll never turn down ripe cantaloupe or fresh strawberries. But bananas in a fruit salad? Not a fan. They get brown and mushy—and everyone avoids them.

Yet those slimy banana bits at the bottom of the fruit bowl are packed with nutrition. When we skip the bananas in favor of the more appealing fruits, we miss out on vitamins and nutrients. And I think we do something similar with the fruit of the Spirit.

Love, joy, peace—we eagerly embrace these spiritual gifts. Kindness, goodness, faithfulness—we're all in! What a beautiful, fulfilling life to be marked by such fruit. But patience? That one is trickier. We might want to be patient, but do we ever truly desire the process of *becoming* patient? In some Bible translations, patience is called "long-suffering." Now, isn't that the banana of the spiritual fruit salad?

Despite being passed over for more palatable choices, bananas are rich in potassium (which helps regulate blood pressure) and dietary fiber (good for digestion) and are a source of vitamin C (boosts immunity) and tryptophan (which helps improve mood). In the same way, patience—or long-suffering—is packed with benefits. God, in his wisdom, gives us opportunities to endure difficulties so we can experience certain benefits.

Patient endurance builds resilience and inner strength. Long-suffering can improve relationships as we grow in empathy, grace, and tolerance, which lead to deeper connections. It also cultivates spiritual wisdom and emotional maturity. In many ways, long-suffering is like a "superfruit" for improving personal growth and deepening our dependence on Jesus. Now, doesn't that sound like a fruit you need?

Patience and long-suffering can feel especially heavy when you're battling anxiety. It's natural to wonder, *Why am I still dealing with this? Why hasn't it gotten any easier?* But maybe a better question is *God, what are you cultivating in me through this?*

So next time you're tempted to push aside the "banana" moments of life, remember: God is growing something good in you right here.

> ### *Inhale Truth*
> God has good things for me
>
> ### *Exhale Trust*
> Even in my suffering.

God, I don't want to skip over the hard things—like patience and long-suffering—that you're using to grow good fruit in me. Help me trust you even when the "banana" moments of life feel messy and uninviting. Teach me to see patience not as something to avoid but as a gift you use to make me stronger and more like you. Amen.

97

For the Forgotten and Overlooked

What is the price of five sparrows—two copper coins?
Yet God does not forget a single one of them. And the very
hairs on your head are all numbered. So don't be afraid;
you are more valuable to God than a whole flock of sparrows.
—LUKE 12:6–7

Have you ever felt forgotten, unloved, or replaceable? Like you didn't matter? Maybe you've felt easily overlooked—even by those who should care for you the most. I know what it's like to think *No one would notice if I weren't here* or to feel like my needs were dismissed or my worth diminished.

These experiences can shape how we see God. If someone who was supposed to protect us failed, we might assume God will do the same. If we've faced rejection, we might believe God will reject us too. But allowing the hurts of humanity to dictate our view of God can cause greater hurt and anxiety in the long run.

This is why it's so important to name our pain, identify where our wounds come from, and honestly ask whether our view of God's love and character has been shaped more by our experiences than by who he truly is.

When human love fails, God's love remains steady. When people reject, God welcomes and redeems. What others might call disposable, God calls chosen and dearly loved.

Zephaniah 3:17 reminds us, "The LORD your God is with you, the Mighty Warrior who saves. He will take great delight in you; in his love he will no longer rebuke you, but will rejoice over you with singing" (NIV).

Psalm 36:7 says, "How priceless is your unfailing love, O God! People take refuge in the shadow of your wings" (NIV).

This is our Lord! The one who knows every detail about you, even the exact number of hairs on your head. He is a good, safe, powerful protector and provider. He understands every wound of your heart and anxiety weighing heavy on your mind. And? Even when life feels messy and hard, God delights in you, sings over you, and invites you into the shelter of his wings. This is how loved you are.

So when you feel anxious, forgotten, or unwanted, anchor yourself in the truth of Scripture. You are known and cherished by God. You are deeply loved and immeasurably valued. Indeed, you are worth more than all the sparrows.

> ### Inhale Truth
> God sees me and knows me.
>
> ### Exhale Trust
> He calls me worthy.

Lord, thank you for seeing me fully and loving me completely. I give you the pain caused by those who haven't loved me the way you do, and I surrender the anxiety attached to it. Help me truly understand that the brokenness of this world is not a reflection of your care for me. Heal my deep wounds and replace the lies with your truth. I need you, and I trust you. Amen.

98

Heart Surgery

I will give you a new heart, and I will put a new spirit in you.
I will take out your stony, stubborn heart and give you a
tender, responsive heart.
—EZEKIEL 36:26

You don't have to fix yourself.

Full stop. Let's read that again: You don't have to fix yourself.

After God's people had gone through a long period of disobedience, judgment, and exile, the Lord spoke through his prophet Ezekiel, emphasizing that he is a God who is faithful to keep his promises and transform his people—even when they've been stubborn and unresponsive. God takes the responsibility of transformation off his people and places it on himself.

"I will give you a new heart," he declares.

Here's what that means: The things in your past that shackle you to shame, the unhealthy habits that plague your days, everything you want to stop but somehow keep on doing—none of that is a stone wall between you and God. Your past mistakes or present anxiety cannot block you from the relentless love of God. Plus, God isn't withholding his goodness until you clean yourself up or fix all your junk.

God knew we couldn't save ourselves, which is why he gave us a Savior! For all of history, people have been trying to claw their way out of self-made graves. (Ever felt like you were in a pit too deep and dark to crawl out of? Raising my hand.) Since the beginning of time, people have tried to follow God only to be swayed by their own sin or others' deception. This is why Scripture says that *all* fall short of the glory of God.[41] It is because of God's mercy and love through Christ Jesus that we have been saved by grace alone.[42]

Do you need a fresh start? A total soul reset? If anxiety feels like stubborn stones around your heart, choking out the joy and peace you long for, there's good news! God's got a new heart waiting for you—heart transplants are his specialty. Tell him you're ready to receive a heart that is tender and responsive to him. Tell him you're ready to exchange your spirit of anxiety for his spirit of peace.

There's no better place to be than in the Healer's hands. If you're ready for heart surgery, so is he. It's time for new life.

Inhale Truth
I don't have to fix myself.

Exhale Trust
God gives me a new heart.

God, I'm so grateful that you don't give up on your people—that you don't give up on me. I don't have to meet an impossible standard to be loved by you. I just have to come. So here I am, ready for heart surgery. You know the places in my heart that are rock-hard or stone-cold. Cut away my anxiety. Fill me with your presence and your peace. I'm ready to be made new in you. Amen.

PEACE
PRACTICE
~14~

Pray

Rejoice in our confident hope.
Be patient in trouble, and *keep on praying*.

—ROMANS 12:12

When anxiety creeps in or feels like a lead blanket you can't take off, prayer is your direct line to God's peace. Prayer helps you release your fears and grab hold of God's comfort.

The prayers in this book are a great place to start, but prayer isn't meant just for certain moments—it's for *every* moment. Try praying through a psalm, letting God's words direct your thoughts and settle your soul.

Shift your focus outward by praying for others. And don't forget to praise God for who he is—faithful, kind, unchanging.

Prayer doesn't need to be long or complicated—it's simply welcoming God into your day, wherever you are. The more you pray, the less space anxiety takes up and the more Jesus's peace will fill every corner of your heart.

99

Who Do You Want to Be?

Let all that I am praise the LORD;
may I never forget the good things he does for me.
—PSALM 103:2

My favorite people are the ones who don't sugarcoat the hard of life but also don't hesitate to praise God in the midst of it. I'm allergic to false positivity, but I am drawn to genuine gratitude.

Some of the most joy-full, peace-filled people I've encountered have endured the greatest struggles: cancer, the loss of a spouse or child, a terminal diagnosis, heart-wrenching betrayal, prejudice, abuse, or extreme injustice. They don't deny the darkness, but they are quick to point to the light.

On the flip side, there are people who have let the injuries and offenses of life lead them to bitterness and resentment. They've stacked every hard thing around their hearts like the bricks of a fortress. And it begs the question: What kind of people are we becoming?

The truth is, we cannot control every circumstance, but we can control our responses. We cannot prevent every bad thing, but we can pursue God's goodness. The primary difference between those who get hardened by life and those who get softer is a posture of praise. The first group complains; the latter calls out God's faithfulness. The first group fixates on *their* wounds, while the latter focuses on Christ who overcame the world by *his* wounds. One sees their scars as evidence of abandonment; the other, as a testimony of God's healing.

We've all got trials in our past and challenges in our present. God is tender toward and mindful of the things that weigh you down and shackle your soul. And he is still writing your story. The enemy wants you to spend your life rehearsing your grievances; Jesus came so your life can reflect his goodness and glory.

The first step to becoming a person of genuine praise is to look for God's fingerprints. See his love. Call out his grace and kindness and every answered prayer. Don't wait for that situation to improve or that relationship to heal. Don't wait for your anxiety to decrease or your depression to lift. Don't wait for the news to be hopeful or your neighborhood to be united. Praise God right now. In this moment.

The more you turn your heart to praise, the more walls will come down. The more you praise God in the darkness, the more his light will shine in.

Inhale Truth
God is good

Exhale Trust
All the time!

God, you are so deserving of my praise! Help me recognize your goodness in my life—from how you formed me in my mother's womb to the breath in my lungs today. Remove any bitterness or resentment within me, and fill my heart with your love and gratitude. Even when my anxiety persists or challenges increase, I will praise you! Your presence sustains me, and your love pours into me. Great is your faithfulness. Amen.

100

The Way Forward

I am the way, the truth, and the life.
—JOHN 14:6

For our final day together, I want to share my heart for you.

I hope this book has been a gentle guide to seeing God's goodness in the midst of your anxiety. As these pages come to an end, continue in the rhythm of reading God's Word, reflecting on his promises, breathing in truth, exhaling your trust, and praying to the God who sees you, knows you, and never stops loving you.

I pray for freedom, healing, and breakthrough in your life as you trust the God of all hope. I pray you tell God the truth about your fears every day so you can receive *his* truth in fear's place.

I pray you know that whatever ties your soul in anxious knots matters to God. *You* matter to God. He is not over you or annoyed by you. He is not disappointed in you, and he'll never give up on you. Your anxiety is not a condemnation but an invitation to deeper intimacy with Jesus.

God's arms are open. You get to come. Come weary and burdened. Come believing or doubting. Come joyful or depressed, worried or content. Just come and keep coming.

You picked up this book looking for a solution to your anxiety—Jesus is the way. You read to the end looking for strength to get through another day—Jesus is the way. You want a light in the darkness, fresh hope for old struggles, new victories for ongoing battles—Jesus is the one and only way.

Come back to this book again and again as a guide to meaningful encounters with God. I pray it becomes a favorite companion on your journey. I pray you will share the prayers with others. Teach your friends, children, and co-workers how the Word of God and the breath he gives can refresh their soul and regulate their nervous system. And I hope you will buy another copy and gift it to someone who is wading through the murky waters of anxiety, so they too will know they're not alone.

But more than anything, I pray you will walk with Jesus. Learn his voice. Follow his leading. Lean on his strength. Trust him to guide every step. And open your heart to receive everything he has for you.

You are so loved.

> *Inhale Truth*
> Jesus is the way.
>
> *Exhale Trust*
> I receive his truth and life.

Jesus, thank you for being the way, the truth, and the life I've always longed for and deeply need today. You are my shepherd and savior, my rock and redeemer, my closest friend. Thank you for each breath I take and the peace in my heart—daily miracles from you. I love you, and I am so grateful to be loved by you. Keep attending to my anxious soul. Your ways are good. Your will be done. Always. Amen.

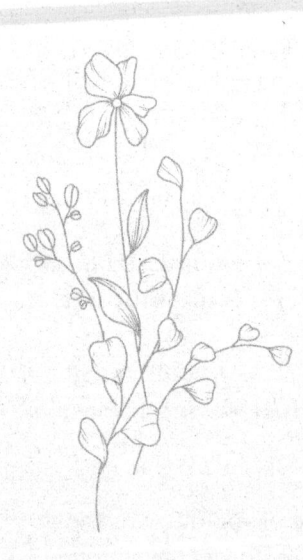

With Gratitude

It's impossible to get to the end of this book and not acknowledge the village who carried me here.

First to my husband, Chris. You ground me when I'm getting swallowed, give me really good advice (even when I don't want it), and always support me. I'm forever grateful for the gift of you.

To my sons, Noah, Elias, and Jude. You blessed me with compassion when my anxiety was high and grace when deadlines loomed heavy. You are my greatest treasures. I pray these pages will be a legacy of hope and healing in your lives.

To my mom, Patty. Thank you for loving me, encouraging me, sharing my books with all your people, and calling out the goodness of God you see in me. Love you, Mama.

To my dad, Ralph. If you were here, I know you'd be really proud of me. And I know the words in this book would have really helped you. So grateful we will meet again—whole and healed in heaven.

To my agent, Kathleen Kerr. A chance meeting at a Red House turned into a kindred connection—how lucky I am to have you in my corner. You are the kindest, wisest, humblest, and most prayerful cheerleader and advocate a writer could ask for. "It only takes the right one."

A huge thank-you to my editor Jamie Lapeyrolerie along with Laura Barker and the entire WaterBrook team. Thank you for championing this message of hope so countless anxious souls can know they're not alone.

Thank you, Jennifer Tucker, for lending your voice to this book. I'm so grateful God crossed our paths through (in)courage all those years ago and has since knit our hearts together as anxiety warriors, sisters in Christ, and friends. It's been an absolute joy to see God use your words to reach multitudes. You are indeed a *writer*!

I'm a woman rich in friendship, so it'd be impossible to name every dear soul who has touched my heart and therefore made an imprint on this book. Yet I must thank Elise, Mindy, Sara, Kimberlee, Kyan, Kathi, Michele, Kaitlyn, Anjuli, and Ligia for being relentless encouragers and prayer warriors. I can't thank you enough.

And of course, my greatest gratitude goes to Jesus. You've met me in the pit of anxiety again and again, loved me there, and carried me out. You truly are my peace, the reason I have hope, and my dearest friend. Partnering with you, Lord, in this ministry of words is one of the greatest honors of my life. Gratitude upon gratitude for your grace upon grace. Your love never fails. Great is your faithfulness.

Notes

1. Luke 18:41.
2. Isaiah 53:3.
3. Steve Graff, "Inside Fear and Its Disorders," Penn Medicine News, October 23, 2018, www.pennmedicine.org/news/news-blog/2018/october/inside-fear-and-its -disorders.
4. 1 Thessalonians 5:17.
5. 2 Corinthians 12:9, csb.
6. Annie Wright, "What Is the Window of Tolerance, and Why Is It So Important?," *Psychology Today,* May 23, 2022, www.psychologytoday.com/us/blog/making-the -whole-beautiful/202205/what-is-the-window-of-tolerance-and-why-is-it-so -important.
7. Romans 5:8.
8. Romans 8:28, niv.
9. Psalm 34:18; Isaiah 40:11; Exodus 3:12; Joshua 1:9; Daniel 3:19–27; 6:19–23; Luke 4:38–39; 8:43–48; John 8:1–11.
10. Luke 24:15, csb.
11. Leo Newhouse, "Is Crying Good for You?," Harvard Health Publishing, March 1, 2021, www.health.harvard.edu/blog/is-crying-good-for-you-2021030122020.
12. Lana Burgess, "Eight Benefits of Crying: Why It's Good to Shed a Few Tears," Medical News Today, updated July 13, 2023, www.medicalnewstoday.com/ articles/319631#benefits-of-crying.
13. National Institute of Mental Health, "Any Anxiety Disorder," www.nimh.nih.gov/ health/statistics/any-anxiety-disorder#part_2579.
14. "A 20-Minute Nature Break Relieves Stress," Harvard Health Publishing, July 1, 2019, www.health.harvard.edu/mind-and-mood/a-20-minute-nature-break -relieves-stress.
15. Ezekiel 37:1, 10.
16. Ezekiel 37:14.

17. A version of this story appears in (in)courage, *Take Heart: 100 Devotions to Seeing God When Life's Not Okay,* ed. Grace Cho and Anna Rendell (Revell, 2020), 86–88.

18. Sarah Young, *Jesus Calling: Enjoying Peace in His Presence* (Thomas Nelson, 2004), 298.

19. M. Petersson, P. Alster, T. Lundeberg, K. Uvnäs-Moberg, "Oxytocin Causes a Long-Term Decrease of Blood Pressure in Female and Male Rats," *Physiology & Behavior* 60, no. 5 (November 1996): 1311–15, https://pubmed.ncbi.nlm.nih.gov/8916187/.

20. Psalm 34:8.

21. Psalm 19:10.

22. John 6:35.

23. Matthew 4:4.

24. "How Laughter Can Relieve Stress + Ideas to Laugh It Off," University of St. Augustine for Health Sciences, accessed April 4, 2025, www.usa.edu/blog/how-laughter-can-relieve-stress/.

25. Luke 6:45.

26. Ephesians 4:31.

27. Romans 5:8.

28. John 4:1–42; Luke 19:1–10; John 5:1–15.

29. Ephesians 6:12.

30. Romans 8:37.

31. Deuteronomy 31:8.

32. Psalm 34:18.

33. "3309. *merimnaó,*" Bible Hub, accessed May 28, 2025, https://biblehub.com/greek/3309.htm.

34. Philippians 4:7.

35. "Cortisol," Cleveland Clinic, last reviewed February 17, 2025, https://my.clevelandclinic.org/health/articles/22187-cortisol.

36. Michael J. Breus, "How Getting Rest Helps Repair Your Brain," *Psychology Today,* May 26, 2020, www.psychologytoday.com/us/blog/sleep-newzzz/202005/how-getting-rest-helps-repair-your-brain.

37. Philippians 4:6–7.

38. Acts 16:22–24.

39. Acts 16:16–19.

40. Acts 16:29–34.

41. Romans 3:23.

42. Ephesians 2:4–5.

About the Author

BECKY KEIFE is a Bible teacher, speaker, and author of books and Bible studies, including *The Simple Difference* and *Create in Me a Heart of Peace*. She loves guiding people in learning to hear God's voice and receive their kingdom identity. Becky is passionate about helping people break free from limiting beliefs and step confidently into their God-given purpose so they can live with greater peace, clarity, and impact. As a dedicated mental health advocate, Becky equips individuals, organizations, and churches to understand anxiety from a biblical perspective and care for people who are struggling. Long naps, puffy clouds, and shady trails make her really happy. Becky resides in Southern California with her husband and three always-hungry teenage sons.

Learn more about Becky's work and invite her to speak at beckykeife.com, or reach out and say hello on Instagram @beckykeife—she'd love to hear how these pages have touched your soul.